Chasing Fireflies

Book Five
Jacob's Daughter series

T0204296

WRITTEN BY
Samantha Jillian Bayarr

PRINTED IN THE UNITED STATES

Livingston Hall Publishers
Samantha Jillian Bayarr
Book FIVE of Jacob's Daughter series

Also by Samantha Jillian Bayarr

LWF Amish Series
Little Wild Flower Book I
Little Wild Flower Book II
The Taming of a Wild Flower
Little Wild Flower in Bloom
Little Wild Flower's Journey

Christian Romance
Milk Maid in Heaven
The Anniversary

Christian Historical Romance
A Sheriff's Legacy: Book One
Preacher Outlaw: Book Two
Cattle Rustler in Petticoats: Book Three

Jacob's Daughter Amish Collection
Jacob's Daughter
Amish Winter Wonderland
Under the Mulberry Tree
Amish Winter of Promises
Chasing Fireflies
Amish Summer of Courage
An Amish Harvest
An Amish Christmas Wish

Companion Series
An Amish Courtship
The Quilter's Son
An Amish Widower
Amish Sisters

Please note: All editions may not be available yet.
Please check online for availability.

Chapter 1

I'm drowning!
Help me!
Rose Graber couldn't say the words she longed to scream. She knew that even if she *could* scream them, there was no one around to hear her, and she had sunk too far to the bottom of the pond for any sound to escape her lips.

Panic seized her as she tried to free her foot from the entanglement of the thick plant roots at the bottom of the murky water.

Blackness surrounded her.

Her conscience had warned her not to borrow the paddle boat, but the temptation had been too strong to resist. The moon was full, and with only a few sparse clouds in the sky, it was the perfect night for a quick boat ride. She'd been careful to place the Mason jar filled with fireflies at the end of the dock to guide her way to a safe return. But even the fireflies couldn't help her now.

Rose tugged, but the plants had a strong hold on her foot. She twisted every which way, unable to break free. Instinct tried desperately to bring air into her lungs, but there was only water. Hopelessness shrouded her as she surrendered to the pull of her fate.

ഇൗരു

Noah Beiler skipped a stone across the large pond, trying to mask his feelings. Even after more than a year, he could not put that day out of his mind. That day changed his life forever; it was the end to his future—his life. Picking up another stone, he leaned sideways and tossed it across the surface of the pond, his anger propelling it further. His eyes followed the smooth, flat stone as it skipped seven times before sinking below the murky depths of the pond in which he despised.

Following the ripples the stone had created on the surface of the water, Noah fixed his eyes on a small paddle boat making its way toward him. Even from that distance, he could see that it was a young woman pedaling the boat that he knew belonged to the Miller B&B. The boat was reserved for guests, and Noah thought it strange that the driver was not an *Englischer*. He continued to watch her for a few minutes from behind the tall willow reeds that grew along the bank.

Intending to avoid being seen, he turned and pointed himself toward home. A loud splash suddenly echoed from behind him. Heart pounding, he turned around, racing back to the water's edge. Straining his eyes to see movement on the water, he caught only the slow-moving wake from the disturbance the splash had caused. Had she fallen in? She was no longer on the boat, and he heard no other sound indicating she was swimming or even struggling.

He scanned the pond one more time.

Nothing.

A paralyzing silence consumed him as he contemplated having to go into the water. His heart was racing and his breathing heaved as he robotically removed his shoes. Tossing them to the ground with shaky hands, he attempted to yell out to her, but no sound escaped him. Fear circulated through him as he stepped off the shore and into the cool water. He waded quickly through the muck on the bottom until he was out far enough to begin swimming. Each stroke he took toward the young woman reminded him of that night—that cold night in November when his whole world fell apart.

Chapter 2

Reaching the boat quickly, Noah grabbed onto the edge and scanned the water's surface for any sign of the young woman. Just as he'd feared, he would have to dive down in the murky depths with only the light of the moon to guide him to her whereabouts. Taking in a deep breath, Noah pushed aside his fear and said a quick prayer as he dove down head first. Moonlight filtered through the water making his journey easier, but he couldn't see the bottom. A rush of bubbles floated up past him from just below where he was, and he knew they had come from the young woman. They may have been her last breath.

Running out of air himself, he surfaced long enough to take another deep breath, then plunged himself toward the bottom of the pond where the young woman awaited his rescue. The further down he swam, the more difficult it was to see, but it was just light enough that he was able to locate her.

Grabbing hold of her limp body, he tried to pull her toward the surface but she was stuck. Knowing he was risking his own air supply, he pushed himself further down to where her foot was tangled. With only his hands to guide him, he separated the plant's roots that imprisoned her, setting her foot free. Cupping his hand under her dainty arm, he pushed off from the bottom of the pond, hoping to surface before his own lungs collapsed.

It seemed a small eternity as he kicked and fluttered his free arm to get to the surface.

Gott help me to hold on just a little longer. The light is getting brighter. I can see the moon.

Noah exploded to the surface, gasping for air as he continued to kick his weary legs to stay afloat. Leaning on his side with the young woman against him above the water, he heaved air into his lungs and kicked a little harder until he closed the short distance between him and the paddle boat. Reaching up with his free arm, he grabbed hold of the side of the boat. He pulled himself up until his arm hung over the side, and then he hoisted her small, water-soaked frame into the boat. Pulling himself up, he climbed on the edge and pushed the young woman onto her side. He thumped his open hand across her back the same as he had over a year ago.

Why wasn't she breathing?

Emma please don't die.

Placing a finger to her throat, he felt a weak pulse. Fighting back tears, he pulled her into his arms and kissed her gently on the cheek before applying light pressure to her ribcage. He knew he had to expel the water from her lungs quickly or he would lose her forever. He'd endured that once already, and he would not let it happen again.

Chapter 3

Rose convulsed, spewing a rush of water from her lungs. She gasped for air; coughing each time she tried to draw air into her lungs. Her eyes fluttered open and closed several times before remaining closed. Noah positioned himself on the opposite seat and began to pedal the small watercraft as fast as his wobbly legs would work. The shore, where he'd been just a short time ago, seemed like it had somehow stretched to double the length it had been when he swam out to rescue the young woman.

Hold on, Emma, don't let go this time.

Rose groaned, tossing her head back and forth a few times, but didn't open her eyes.

Noah grabbed her hand. "Stay with me, Emma. We're almost there."

As soon as the boat hit the bottom of the pond, Noah jumped out and yanked it ashore. Then he reached in and pulled Rose into his arms and carried her up the bank.

She wriggled in his grasp. "Put me down."
Noah looked at her, shock in his eyes as she
began to smack at his chest with her open hand.
"I said, put me down!"
He attempted to set her down and she stumbled
backward, landing in the grass.
"I'm sorry," he said. "I didn't mean to drop
you, but you were wiggling so much I couldn't hold
onto you."
Rose examined her soaking wet dress, and then
looked up into Noah's eyes. She studied him for a
minute. His hair was long and wavy, and rested on his
shoulders. His jaw line was covered in a line of
neatly-trimmed whiskers, yet he wore traditional
Amish clothing.
"Did I hear you call me Emma?"
Noah's face drained of all color. He hadn't
realized he'd said it.
"You fell into the water. You were stuck down
in the muck at the bottom of the pond, but I pulled
your leg free. I'm sorry if I called you Emma. I guess
I was a little disoriented and thought you were
someone else."
Rose's eyes grew wide. "The boat! I have to
take it back to the B&B."
She jumped up from the ground and started to
walk, but collapsed in the grass again, her legs too
weak to hold her up so soon.
Noah took a step toward her, but she verbalized
a warning.

"If you come any closer, I'll scream. My *schweschder* will hear you and so will her beau. He's strong."

Noah stood his ground. "I don't want to hurt you. I pulled you out of the pond. If I hadn't, you would have drowned. Are you alright?"

"I'm a little dizzy, and I feel like I can't get enough air."

Noah crouched down on his haunches so he wouldn't tower over her any longer. He hoped the gesture would make her feel safe.

"You need to cough up the rest of the water that got into your lungs. If you don't, pneumonia could set in."

Rose leered at him. "Are you a doctor?"

"*Nee,* but *mei grossdaddi* is. He taught me a lot until…" his voice trailed off, and Rose didn't care to press him for more information.

Rose pushed her damp hair off her face; her *kapp* hanging precariously from her neck by the ribbons. "I need to go home before my *familye* starts to look for me."

Noah held a hand out to her and she took it, allowing him to assist her to a wobbly standing position. Her teeth were chattering, and water dripped from her dress.

"Can I get you a blanket?" he pointed behind her. "My *haus* is right there.

Rose turned around and looked at the dilapidated home. Overgrown weeds covered most of the yard, except for a narrow path leading to the embankment. The shutters were crooked, and she could see by the moonlight that it was in desperate need of a *gut* white-wash.

Noah could see the apprehension in her eyes. Who could blame her? He hadn't done anything to preserve the home for the past year and one half. He'd merely existed there—a shell of a *mann*.

He took a step toward the path and called over his shoulder. "It'll only take a minute. I'll be right back."

Rose watched him disappear into the thick weeds, and couldn't decide whether to wait or make a run for it. But she was cold, and the thought of having a blanket would buy her enough time to dry off before returning home to Katie and all her inquisitiveness.

Noah returned quickly, offering her a wool blanket one might use for a horse. Didn't the *mann* own any soft quilts?

She shied away from him when he tried to drape it over her shoulders, so he handed it to her.

"*Danki,*" she said as she ran toward the boat.

"Wait," he called after her.

It was too late for him to stop her. She had already pushed the craft into the water and hopped in. She pedaled away quickly, and Noah wasn't willing to go back into the unyielding water.

Chapter 4

Noah set out on foot, walking along the pond's edge, keeping track of the young woman's course.

He feared for her safety, and prayed that he wouldn't have to go in and rescue her a second time. It was the second time he had said a prayer on the young woman's behalf. Praying had become strange to him—a thing of the past, as he had not uttered a single prayer since the night Emma had left him.

When Rose pulled up to the dock at the B&B, the light from the jar of fireflies had become dim, and Noah was waiting for her there. Grabbing the rope, he towed her to the edge and tied up the boat without saying a word to her.

She looked at him, moonlight accentuating her milky smooth skin. He longed to reach out and touch her, but suppressed the notion, wondering why he felt such a pull toward the young woman.

"Why are you following me?"

Noah gulped. "I'm not. I only wanted to make certain you would make it back safely."

"I'm here now so you can go. *Danki* for pulling me out of the water, but I think we should both go back home."

She brushed past him, pulling the itchy wool blanket around her shoulders.

"Wait," he called after her a second time. "I don't even know your name."

She hesitated, considering telling him, but then decided against it. She walked away without saying a word. She knew it wasn't polite, but she couldn't have him knowing who she was or he'd go straight to Caleb's *aenti* and tell her she'd taken the boat without permission. It was better to stay away from the strange *mann* whom she couldn't even be sure was Amish.

ৰ০৫৪

Noah dragged his bare feet through the cool grass as he trudged back toward his *haus*. The moon shone brightly, lighting the way, but he knew the path well. The humidity level had prevented his clothing from drying even a little bit, and so he still dripped and sloshed as he walked. When he reached the spot where he'd carelessly tossed aside his shoes, he collapsed in the grass beside them. He looked out across the smooth, glassy surface of the water that reflected the moonlight, and let out a long sigh. He'd managed to save her—the young woman he'd mistakenly called *Emma.* Had he gone mad after all this time? Or had the stress of the event brought him too close to his own reality? Noah cupped his hands over his face and began to weep as he prayed. *Danki, dear Gott, for helping me save her.*

༄༅

Rose felt the shock of what happened to her as she slipped under the warm quilt in her *Aenti* Nettie's old room. After *Aenti's* marriage to Hiram Miller, the woman offered to let her come back and stay for the summer with her *schweschder,* Katie, whom she'd given the *haus* to as an early present for her upcoming wedding. Since her *aenti* moved into Elder Miller's *haus,* she and her *schweschder* had the whole *haus* to themselves.

But tonight, Rose wasn't happy to be all alone in this strange room. She had avoided Katie, who'd sat on the porch swing with her beau, Caleb. Rose had sneaked in through the kitchen so she wouldn't have to explain how her clothes had gotten all wet.

If *Gott* was teaching her a lesson for borrowing the boat without permission, she felt it rather harsh for a punishment that she should nearly drown. Or it was possible that she shouldn't have leaned over so far to get a closer look at the frogs on the lily pads. Either way, whether it was a lesson or her own fault, she had to make it right.

I'll put the money for the boat rental in a jar and leave it tomorrow if that will bring redemption. Forgive me dear Gott. And please bless the mann who saved me. If I didn't know better, I'd think he was the one who needed saving just as much as I did. Danki for sparing my life. I am your servant. Please direct me to do your wille.

Rose drifted off into a restless sleep, filled with dreams of being trapped beneath the surface of the murky pond water—until her handsome rescuer took her into his arms and—kissed her? Rose rolled over and groaned as she opened her eyes to the little bit of sunshine filtering in through the sheer curtains on her window. How had morning come so quickly? And why had she dreamed that the *mann* who pulled her from pond had kissed her?

Chapter 5

Rose dressed quickly and straightened her hair, pinning on a clean *kapp* and tying the ribbons at her neckline. She wanted to get a head-start on morning chores so she would have time to explore the surrounding area before it turned too warm.

Once outside, the chickens clucked impatiently for their grain. When she exited the barn with a full bucket of grain for the hungry yard-birds, Caleb pulled his buggy into the drive near the kitchen door. Rose stood back and watched her *schweschder* run to him and kiss him full on the mouth. Rose had never had a kiss from a *mann* and wasn't sure if she ever would. She was older than Katie, who would be married in November.

She held back near the barn for a minute and waited for the two of them to notice she was standing there and stop with their mushiness. When it became obvious they were not going to notice her anytime soon, Rose cleared her throat as she approached the happy couple, who seemed oblivious to the world around them. Katie backed away from Caleb, her cheeks turning pink. "*Gudemariye*, Rose. Did you sleep well? I didn't hear you come in last night." Rose pursed her lips. "That's because you were too busy with Caleb. Doesn't he ever stay home?" Katie raised an eyebrow at her older *schweschder.* "That's not a very kind thing to say." Rose began to toss feed to the chickens who were clucking relentlessly at her feet.

"I came here to spend the summer with my *schweschder,* and I've been here almost a month already and have had to entertain myself because you are too busy with Caleb. I thought you wanted me here to help you plan the wedding. We've barely gotten anything done, and there is still so much to do before I go back home."

Caleb was busy retrieving tools from the back of his buggy and could not hear their conversation. Still, Katie felt unnerved that Rose was voicing dislike for her betrothed so openly.

"Why do you dislike Caleb?"

Rose's look softened. "I don't dislike him. I only dislike the amount of time you spend with him. I haven't had a single moment with you since I've been here."

"I'm here now. What would you like to do today?"

Rose bristled. "Why is he here?"

"He's here to fix the barn door so it latches correctly, and the hole in the side where the wood has decayed. *Aenti* hired him to take care of these things before the foxes come and make a meal of our chickens."

Rose suddenly felt selfish. What right did she have to demand her *schweschder's* time away from her betrothed? They had overcome some great obstacles to be together, and they deserved to be happy.

"I'm sorry, Katie, for sounding like a selfish *boppli.*"

Katie hugged Rose. "You're right about me neglecting you since you've been here. You came here to help me before I have to go back to teaching in the fall, and I've already wasted your first few weeks here."

"I know you want to spend as much time with him as possible. I'd probably be the same way if I had a beau. But since that isn't likely, I'm taking it out on you."

Katie felt badly for her *schweschder*. "Don't say such things, Rose. You never know what *Gott* has in store for your life. And here I was envying you for being so independent."

"Why would you envy me? Independent is a kinder word for lonely spinster with no prospects."

Katie fought the lump forming in her throat. "You will find someone; I just know it."

Rose hated to admit it, but she may have already stumbled upon someone who had caught her interest. He was a little rough around the edges, and perhaps a little unkempt, but with the right woman in his life, he could change. Couldn't he?

Rose chided herself for thinking such things about the *mann* who had—saved her life. Rose sank to the grass, the reality of what happened last night hitting her suddenly.

Katie crouched down beside her. "Rose, is something wrong?"

The hens swarmed to the feed bucket that had tipped out its contents onto the ground when Rose collapsed.

Rose waved off her *schweschder's* concerns. "I think I got a little dizzy for a minute. I'm *gut.*"

"You don't look very *gut.* You look pale. Are you ill?"

Rose was trying to sort out how she felt about nearly drowning the night before. She'd come very close until the handsome stranger had rescued her. She'd run off without even catching his name. He'd asked for hers, but she'd ignored him. Why had she acted so rashly? Was she in shock? Was she still in shock now?

"Maybe I should have had more than a glass of milk before coming out in the hot sun. I can't believe how warm it is already. Usually it doesn't get this warm until the middle of July."

Katie called for Caleb who was only a few feet from them.

"Help me get Rose over to the shade of the tree."

A hand-crafted wooden bench sat beneath the tree that held two birdhouses. A set of birds twittered overhead while Katie and Caleb assisted Rose to the waiting bench.

Rose looked out over the expanse of the yard toward Goose Pond. From this distance, she could scarcely see the disheveled house at the opposite end of the water's edge.

Rose looked to Caleb. "Who's the *mann* who lives across the pond in the *haus* with all the overgrown brush?"

Caleb sat next to Katie at the opposite end of the bench. "That *haus* has been abandoned for over a year now. The brush is so overgrown you can barely see the barn anymore."

Rose squinted her eyes. "Are you sure?"

"*Jah,* I'm sure. My cousin, Noah, bought it two years ago. But he's gone now. Did you see someone there?"

"I thought I did, but maybe I was wrong."

Caleb rubbed his hands together thoughtfully.

"It's a tragic story, really. Noah bought that *haus* for his betrothed as a surprise for their wedding. But she never got to live there."

Rose leaned in so she wouldn't miss a single bit of the story. "What happened?"

"The night before their wedding, they went out skating on the pond. The ice was too thin and she drowned. He couldn't save her. It destroyed him— especially since her *familye* blamed Noah for letting her go out onto the thin ice. He left the community with no word."

Rose's heart nearly leaped from her ribcage.

"No one has seen him since then?"

"*Jah.* The *haus* has remained vacant out of respect. We have all hoped he would someday return to the community. His *daed,* my *onkel,* has been so worried about him this whole time. Especially since Noah's *mamm* died just a couple of years before he lost his betrothed. This has been very difficult for his *daed* to first lose my *aenti,* and now my cousin. But no one has seen Noah since the funeral."

"What was the name of his betrothed?" Rose asked slowly.

Caleb looked up at her. "Her name was Emma."

Rose felt the blood drain from her face.

"What's wrong?" Katie asked. "You look like you've seen a ghost."

Rose jumped up and tested her legs for stability before she took off. "I *may* have."

Chapter 6

Rose stepped into the yard of the disheveled *haus* looking for any sign that the *mann* who had rescued her was real. Feeling a little unnerved about being in his yard, she considered if she should wade through the tall grass and weeds to gain access to the door. She wasn't sure how brave she felt at the moment, especially since the reality of her near-drowning had just hit her full-on. Katie had tried to run after her, but Rose had always been a fast runner. She'd called over her shoulder for her *schweschder* not to worry, but she couldn't be sure Katie had heard her. It was too late to worry about it now. She was standing on the edge of a property that belonged to a *mann* who might very well be dead—the *mann* who'd saved her from drowning last night.

৪৩৫৪

Noah sat at his kitchen table drinking a cup of *kaffi* when he noticed the young woman whom he'd rescued the night before enter his yard. Why had she come here? He'd managed to keep himself hidden away from the entire community all this time, and now she was about to expose him. He still didn't feel ready to face them after failing to save his beloved Emma. He'd managed to cut himself off from the community and remain secluded in the fortress he'd allowed to grow around him, and he wasn't about to let a pretty woman ruin it for him.

He considered remaining in the *haus,* but he worried she might try to peer into the windows. She would surely see him then since his Emma had never had the chance to adorn the windows or any other part of the *haus* with her talent for sewing.

He'd had his moment of weakness last night when he'd kissed the young woman's cheek and held her in his arms. But it was time to put his feelings back on the shelf where they belonged. He had no right to any kind of happiness as long as Emma lay cold in the ground.

ॐ

Rose wandered around toward the pond, noting the deep grooves in the mud where the paddle boat had been pushed aground. It was evident that she had been here, but there was no sign of the *mann* that Caleb had called Noah. Had she imagined him? Was he gone like Caleb said, or had he meant that Noah was also dead? If she'd imagined him, then how had she gotten out of the lake?

Standing at the edge of the pond, she looked out over the water. This pond had taken a life, and had almost taken hers. Was it her own carelessness that had caused the accident, or had it been *Gott* who'd orchestrated the events as a way of opening her eyes to something?

Show me what you want from me, Gott. If this is all part of your plan, please give me the courage to endure your wille for the sake of your purpose.

A rustling sound from behind startled her out of her reverie.

As she turned around, she saw *Noah*. The sun was directly behind him, but she could see that it was him. She held up a hand to shield her eyes from the bright sun.

Rose took a step toward him. "Are you Noah?"

Noah couldn't help but feel drawn to her, but he pushed his feelings down. She was even prettier than he'd thought last night. Her dark blond hair was pinned back neatly, but little wisps of hair fluttered across her cheeks in the gentle breeze. He had no right to delight in the depths of her hazel eyes that sparkled when she smiled.

Why is she smiling at me? She shouldn't be here. I can't be trusted. I let my poor Emma down, and it's only a matter of time before this lovely creature finds out that I failed to save her. And then she will despise me like Emma's familye.

"Why are you here?"

"I came to see if you're real. Or if I imagined you last night."

Noah was not prepared for such a question, and had to admit he'd begun to wonder the same thing himself lately. He'd kept himself secluded for so long, that it was strange hearing his name spoken.

"I think you imagined me," he surprised himself by saying.

Rose stepped forward and placed her hand on his forearm. "I'm not imaging that. Are you?"

Noah shook his head. The feel of her warm hand on his arm sent a shiver of longing through him. He had denied himself of all contact with any others in the community for too long. He'd been punishing himself for not being able to save Emma. He knew she would not want him to deprive himself the way he'd been doing for more than a year, but it was what he felt he deserved for being the one to live when she had died.

Noah flicked his arm away from her grasp.

"You should go. And don't tell anyone you saw me here."

"What about your *familye?* They would be happy to see you haven't left the community. I know your cousin, Caleb, would. He said so just a few minutes ago."

Anger showed in Noah's eyes. "You told him I was here?"

"*Nee,* but you should. He's worried about you."

Noah scowled. "No one is worried about me. If you didn't tell him I was here, how is it that you know my name?"

Rose jutted out her chin. "I only asked who lived here."

Noah's expression turned dark. "No one is to know I am here, do you understand? I am dead to them."

Rose left the stubborn *mann,* determined never to talk to him again. What had she been thinking when she saw him as kind and handsome? She'd been a fool to see him as anything more than a coward who refused to face his biggest enemy—fear.

Chapter 7

Noah felt empty and alone as he watched the young woman leave his property. He still hadn't learned her name, but it was probably for the best. If he knew her name, it would make things personal between them, and that's the last thing he wanted.

Wasn't it?

He didn't need any complications in his life. His life was just fine before she came along. No one bothered him. He didn't have to answer to anyone. But most of all, there was nothing to remind him of what he'd been missing.

Until now.

Noah had done all he could to remain focused on avoiding his community. So why did this young woman suddenly make him want to change his mind? Loneliness was not a *gut* enough reason; there had to be more to it than that. Was *Gott* prompting him to help her beyond pulling her out of the pond?

Whatever it was, he decided he would keep a look-out for her—just in case.

ෝලෝ

"Where were you?" Katie demanded. "I've been worried about you."

Rose dabbed at the sweat on her brow with her apron. "I had to clear something up in my head, but I'm fine now. I'm sorry to have worried you. But really, you can see that I am fine."

Katie narrowed her eyes. "If you're really *fine,* why do you keep saying it? Is there something you don't want to tell me?"

Rose forced a smile. "I am the older *schweschder,* and I'm telling you everything is fine. Why don't we get a little *kaffi* so we can begin planning your wedding?"

Katie's face lit up. "I have a better idea. Let's go to the bakery and sit with Rachel. She will make us *kaffi,* and we can discuss everything over a fresh batch of the best cookies I have ever tasted. Now that I'm going to be part of the *familye,* Rachel has agreed to give me the recipe as a wedding gift."

Rose shook her head. "Nothing is better than *mamm's* snickerdoodles."

"You will take back that statement when you taste these cookies. But never tell *mamm* there is a better cookie out there than hers."

They both giggled as they walked toward the barn to hitch up the buggy.

෨෮

Lillian's Bakery was abuzz with plenty of customers, both Amish and *Englisch*. Rose was impressed with Caleb's *schewschder's* ability to handle each and every one of them so quickly and efficiently. Rose had given some serious consideration to the summer job at the B&B, and watching Rachel move about the bakery enjoying her work was enough to convince her. Caleb's *aenti* was in need of help since her current employee had to go back to Lancaster for the rest of the summer to be with a sick relative, and so she had offered the position to Rose first thing. Rose hoped it wouldn't be too late to accept the offer.

When the last customer was served and happily on her way, Rachel motioned for Katie and Rose to sit at one of the tables along the front wall of the lobby. She brought *kaffi* and three cups, and then sat down across from Rose.

"I'm so happy to see you made it back, Rose. I'm sorry I've been stuck here and haven't had a chance to visit yet. Caleb tells me you might be working at the B&B for the remainder of the summer."

Rose smiled. "*Jah*, I just now decided to take the position. After watching you bustle around here helping customers, I figure I can clean rooms and wash linens. It should be fun and a lot easier than your job, *nee?*"

"*Jah,* it does get a little busy in here sometimes, but I've finally gotten used to it. I felt like a *dummkopf* when I first started here. Ask Katie how many times she had to help me clean up the kitchen. All it took was a little organization, and I was in business with a full customer load. I really like this job, and it may be my own business soon."

Rose took a sip of her *kaffi*. "*Das wunderbaar.* But Katie promised me you bake the best cookies I could ever taste."

Rachel laughed. "Katie is the best form of advertisement I could ever have. She tells so many people about my cookies I can scarcely keep up with the orders sometimes."

Rachel disappeared into the kitchen and returned quickly with a plateful of frosted cookies and set them on the table in front of Rose, offering her the first one.

Rose sank her teeth into the moist sugar cookie, enjoying a burst of flavor. "Oh my, I *have* to know what you put in this frosting to make it so *wunderbaar.*"

Rachel winked at Katie. "I'm sorry but that is privileged information. I can't give out such an old *familye* recipe to everyone who asks. If I did, it would put me out of business because everyone would be able to make them for themselves. Keeping it a secret is what keeps my customers coming back."

Rose giggled. I suppose you're right, but that doesn't mean I like it. You can count on me as a regular customer."

Rachel smiled. "And that is how I keep customers wanting more. But because you're Katie's *schweschder,* I will give you a discount."

Rose laughed. "I suppose that's fair enough. *Danki,* Rachel."

Katie set down her empty cup. "We didn't come here just for the cookies. We also want to discuss plans for my wedding to your *bruder.*"

Rachel poured herself a second cup of *kaffi.*

"I won't be able to help with weeding the celery patch or anything else that requires me to leave the bakery. But I am more than happy to help with sewing and list-making in-between serving customers."

"I can let you know what my work schedule will be at B&B as soon as I talk to Bess Miller. But I'd enjoy keeping up the celery patch since I prefer being outdoors."

Rose had already noticed Katie's celery patch overlooked Noah's place across the pond, and she was just as interested in keeping an eye on him as she was in keeping the celery free from weeds.

Chapter 8

Rose swallowed hard, determined to get this over with before she lost her nerve.

"There's something I need to confess before I take the job, Miss Miller. You may not want to hire me after you hear what I have to say."

Bess narrowed her brow. "If you are going to work for me, you're going to have to start calling me by my first name. I'm too old to be called *Miss* anymore, and I was never a *Missus,* so Bess will do just fine. And I already know you borrowed my boat last night. And I know that you nearly got yourself drowned. If it weren't for Noah pulling you out of the water, we wouldn't be having this conversation."

Rose felt weak in the knees. "But how…"

"Awhile back I had a critter getting into my garden, and I didn't know how to defend myself against the damage it was causing. So I borrowed a pair of binoculars from *mei bruder,* and that's how I saw everything...right down to the kiss he placed on your cheek."

Rose could feel her cheeks heat up.

He really did kiss me! The nerve of him!

"You know he's here, instead of gone like everyone thinks?"

"I saw you go over there again this morning. I've known he was here all this time. I've been waiting for something or someone to bring him out of that *haus* and make him want to start living again. I saw the way he looked at you this morning. You haven't seen the last of him."

"What if I don't want to see him anymore?"

Bess placed her hands on her broadened hips. "I think it'd be a shame if you never talked to him again. He hasn't had an interest in talking to anyone in over a year. He needs help, and it seems *Gott* has already placed you in Noah's path."

Rose was too embarrassed to speak.

"The job is yours if you want it. I'll even let you take the paddle boat out anytime you like. But only on the condition that you wear the life vest I keep under the seat."

Rose couldn't resist such an offer. If she'd known there was a floatation device on the boat last night, she would have used it. But maybe things were just as Bess had said, and she was meant to fall in the pond—for Noah's sake.

Bess gave Rose a tour of the B&B, and pointed out her duties. She would have two days off per week, which was the perfect amount of time she needed to keep up with the celery patch for Katie's wedding.

ജാരു

Noah looked around at the mess that was his yard. When he'd purchased the *haus*, he'd envisioned the beautiful flowers and over-sized garden Emma would have here. There would be white linen curtains flapping in the breeze from open windows, and there would be bed linens drying on the clothesline. Chickens would hover around her as she threw feed to them every morning, and even their milking cow would greet her happily for the morning milking. He would gracefully tell her to let him do the milking, and she would gently encourage him to spend his time instead on building a cradle for their firstborn. But none of that would happen now. She was gone, and there was no getting her back.

Noah's thoughts took a sudden turn to the young woman, whose life he'd saved. Was it possible that *Gott* had sent her to him for a reason? It had always come naturally for him to accept that everything happened for a reason, but now he found that he second-guessed every decision he made.

Except for last night.

He hadn't thought twice about diving into the water of the pond to save her. He did what needed to be done without any consideration for his own worries. They'd been there on the surface, but he'd done what was needed to do for *her* sake.

Using the sickle he'd brought from the barn, he began to clear the top layer of the thick brush that masked the property. As he made his way toward the pond, he realized that if he cleared all of it, someone might notice. Not yet ready for the community to know he was here, he stopped a few feet short of the edge of the pond.

After working for more than an hour in the warm afternoon sun, Noah had cleared a fair portion of the thick grass and weeds to the point that he could see over the tops of them. He knew it would take several more hours of work before he would have it trimmed to a reasonable length that was suitable for a yard. He'd made some progress. Not nearly enough, but that would come in time. For now, he was satisfied with the improvement that such a seemingly insignificant change had brought.

Knowing it was already late in the season, he decided he'd spend the day tomorrow breaking ground for a garden. With a lot of care, he would still be able to grow tomatoes, peas and potatoes. His root cellar was nearly empty, and he would need to go after food if he didn't grow some. He'd caught a few rabbits and made stew with the root vegetables he had, but even those stores were thinning. The strawberries and raspberries that grew wild alongside the barn were blooming, and he knew that no matter what, he was resourceful enough to keep from going hungry. But would he be able to do that much longer without having to mingle among the community?

Chapter 9

Rose pushed her arms into the life vest and tied the straps. Some might consider her a *dummkopf* for going back out onto the water so soon after nearly drowning, but she had always been one to face her fears directly. Her heart raced a little at the thought of being vulnerable out on the water alone, but she would not let the fear paralyze her. With shaky hands, Rose placed the jar full of freshly-caught fireflies onto the end of the dock, and then slipped the rope off the post. Taking a deep breath, she uttered a quick prayer before stepping into the paddle boat. She sat there for several minutes working up the nerve to pedal out into the open water.

"Are you going to just sit there, or are you planning on leaving the dock?"

Startled by the voice, Rose looked up to see Noah standing at the end of the dock. Eyeing his bare feet let her know why she hadn't heard him approach. His presence was enough to convince her to start pedaling.

Noah lifted his foot and placed it against the side of the paddle boat, giving it a gentle shove.

Rose pursed her lips as she pedaled backward until she was clear from the end of the dock. She moved the lever to turn the rudder, and began to pedal forward. She moved slowly out into the open water, moonlight illuminating the way. Though she was a little frightened, she was glad to be away from Noah, who seemed to have a way of getting under her skin with one simple question—a question she answered only by her actions.

Resisting the urge to look back toward the dock to see if Noah was still standing there, Rose kept her eyes focused on the opposite end of the pond, which was her goal. She wasn't sure if she thought it was odd that Noah should sneak up on her the way he did, or if he was somehow looking out for her.

Rose forced herself to follow the same path she had the night before. She hoped that if she could get all the way across the pond and back, she would be rid of the fear that gripped her.

Gott, please bless me with enough courage to make this journey across the pond and back without falling apart.

ഇൻരു

Noah wasn't sure if he should follow along the edge of the pond to keep a better eye on the young woman, or if he should stay where he was. As he watched her leave the dock, he realized she seemed to be heading straight out into the middle of the pond toward the opposite bank. If he set out on foot, he could meet her at the other end, but from this vantage point, he could more easily see her.

Gott, please place a hedge of protection around her. Bring her back to the dock safely.

Realizing that praying was all he could do for her frustrated him. It was hard for him to trust in *Gott's wille* for himself. He'd trusted his entire life, and it seemed his biggest prayer had gone unanswered. Or had it? He'd had the opportunity to love and be loved, but he never got the chance to have a *familye* of his own. Could it be that *Gott* had other plans for his life? Plans that he'd been too consumed with grief to see? Was it time to put his past behind him and move forward in *Gotte's wille* for his life? He'd certainly been ignoring the gentle prompting up until last night when he'd jumped into the pond and saved the young woman.

What was *Gott* trying to tell him now? And why was he following the young woman's every move as though she was now his responsibility?

Noah lowered himself onto the end of the dock and let his bare feet dangle over the edge, his toes lightly touching the cool water. Listening to the gentle swish of the boat as the blades pushed through the water, he looked up to see that the young woman was already pedaling back toward the dock. He lifted the jar of fireflies from beside him and examined it. The lid was screwed on tightly, and the insects inside seemed to be slowing down from lack of air. Their glowing ends began to dim, and he felt sorry for them. They no longer floated around the jar. Instead, they piled on top of each other at the bottom fighting for space.

Noah looked out across the pond, noting how close the young woman was to the dock already. Opening the lid, he gave the jar a gentle shake, releasing the fireflies out over the water. Their tails lit up as they flew out over the expanse of open water.

He'd freed them just in time.

The young woman pedaled the boat up to the dock, bumping it as she tried to navigate it gracefully back into its spot. Noah stood up and took hold of the rope, tying it around the post. The young woman exited the small water craft, and then stood on the end of the dock, her fists planted firmly on her narrow hips.

"Why did you let my fireflies go?"

Noah took a step backward, wondering if she wanted to take a swing at him. "They were dying."

Rose fumed. "I was going to let them go when I got back to the dock. You could have waited five minutes longer."

Noah couldn't help but smile at her fury. She was cute when she was mad.

"I wasn't certain they would last another second in that jar. Besides, you were close enough to the dock that you could see your way safely."

"And what if I hadn't been? Are you going to follow me around making sure I don't fall in the pond again? I wore a life vest so you can go home and stop spying on me."

Noah turned to go, but then turned back toward her. "Will you at least tell me your name?"

"*Nee,*" she blurted out. "You have no use for knowing my name. I appreciate you being there to save me last night, but now I want you to leave me alone and stop following me."

She brushed past Noah, storming off the dock, and didn't look back.

Chapter 10

Noah knew exactly what he was risking when he drove his buggy into town to purchase some chickens from the feed store, but he kept his hat pulled down over his face and didn't intend on making eye contact with anyone if he could help it. It was time to start bringing his small farm back to life, and the chickens would be a nice start. Not to mention the fact that his stomach would appreciate having eggs on a regular basis, and eventually, a plateful of fried chicken.

The last time he'd gone into town, he'd purchased several bales of hay for his horse along with enough bags of feed to get him through the winter. He knew it was time to pick up a few things for Silo, who'd been his only companion since he'd closed himself off from the community. Truth be told, he'd missed his *familye* and simple conversation. But he still wasn't sure if he was ready for all of that yet. It was tough enough talking to the young woman.

Getting out the few sentences he'd said to her was one of the most difficult things he'd had to do in a long time. He could only imagine how much harder it would be on the day when he finally faced his *familye*.

Given the length of his hair and the trim of his whiskers, he doubted anyone would converse with him. They might assume he was a Mennonite convert, or worse, that he'd been shunned. For all he knew, he *had* been shunned—especially since he hadn't attended church service for more than a year. It wasn't as though he hadn't thought about it; he'd wanted to go and reach out to *familye* and friends, but the longer he stayed away, the easier it was to remain hidden.

After selecting a half-dozen Rhode Island Reds, Noah placed his order for chicken feed and horse chow. It would be all he would be able to carry this trip to town. Already in his head, he was planning a second trip, which really surprised him. But for some reason, *Gott* seemed to be pushing him to make some changes.

As he steered his buggy away from the feed store, he thought he heard someone calling his name.

ഇൽൽ

Rose tossed the sheet over the top of the bed at the B&B, letting it rise above the mattress and fall in a puff of slow-motion freshness. She reveled in the fresh aroma of the line-dried linens, as she made the beds for the incoming guests. She'd already beaten the braided rugs and scrubbed the planked, wooden floors. A little light dusting, and she would be finished with this portion of her duties. Bess had advised her that her days off would depend on the schedule of guests, rather than on specific days. She was agreeable to such a flexible schedule, knowing it would afford her the time she needed to spend with Katie and Rachel planning the wedding.

Her thoughts drifted to Noah, and she wondered if he would show up again this evening when she took her boat ride. Part of her wanted him to be there and was even eager to see him, but another part warned her not to get too friendly with the *mann,* who seemed to be running from *Gott.* Although he'd been kind and even patient with her, he'd closed himself off from the community for a very long time. She couldn't even be sure he was ready to reach out to anyone other than her, and that felt like a very heavy burden for her to carry.

She'd prayed about the situation for some time before finally falling asleep last night, and she was still waiting on an answer. It concerned her that she found him attractive, especially since she did not think he would find her attractive. Katie had always been the pretty *schweschder.* She didn't consider herself unattractive, but she knew she was plain in comparison to most other women. She saw herself as having no striking features or special talents that would make her a smart choice for a *mann.*

Rose wasn't especially talented in the kitchen, and her gardening skills were lacking. It surprised her when Katie had agreed to allow her to tend the celery patch. The real reason she could see was that her younger *schweschder* looked up to her. It made her feel better knowing that Katie trusted her with such an important task, but she couldn't help but wonder how it would feel to prepare for a wedding of her own.

Allowing her thoughts to drift back to Noah, Rose wondered what marriage to such a handsome *mann* would be like. The thought of it brought heat to her cheeks. She chided herself when reality reminded her that he had loved Emma so deeply that he'd abandoned everything to mourn her. She wondered if any *mann* would ever love *her* that deeply.

Chapter 11

"I'm telling you, Katie, it was him. I know it was."

Rose sat down at the table, placing the freshly-baked biscuits in front of her. "Who are you talking about, Caleb?"

He grabbed a biscuit and dropped it on his plate. "My cousin, Noah. I saw him in town at the feed store. When I called out to him, he took off so fast, I couldn't catch up to him."

Rose didn't know much about the *mann,* but she knew enough about Noah to realize he didn't want anyone knowing he was still in the area. He'd made that very clear to her. She'd never known the depth of grief he'd experienced, so she couldn't judge whether it was normal for him to want to be so secluded. For whatever his reasons were, she felt they should be honored until he was ready. It dawned on her that he had tried several times to reach out to her, and she'd rejected his company.

Suddenly feeling shame for her actions, she felt the need to keep his secret. "I'm certain you *think* you saw him because we were talking about him yesterday. Maybe part of you *wanted* for it to be him. But you said yourself; no one has seen him since the funeral. Wherever he is, when he's ready, he will come home."

Caleb let his face drop. "I suppose you're right. I just wish I knew if he was alright. His *daed* is worried about him."

Rose ignored the rest of the conversation, nodding occasionally to make it look like she was participating. She finished her dinner quickly, eager to go the dock at the B&B—eager to see Noah.

After the dishes were washed, she counted on Katie being preoccupied with Caleb. It was such a warm night, they might even take a buggy ride. With the two of them out of the way, Rose was free to go.

ဆာင်

Noah was unsure of himself. Unsure if he should leave the small token with a note, or if he should wait for the young woman to show up so he could give it to her in person. She'd made it clear that she wanted him to leave her alone, but he felt drawn to her in a way he could not explain. As he turned to leave, she wandered up to the dock.

"Noah."

All she said was his name, but it was enough to make him smile. "I brought something for you."

He handed her the square of cheesecloth, and she looked at him with confusion.

"If you put it on the top of the Mason jar in place of the lid, you can still twist the ring over the opening. This way, the fireflies will be able to last long enough for you to pedal the boat from one end of the pond and back again. When you return, their glow will still be very strong, and you will be able to release them unharmed."

Rose looked down at the cheesecloth in her hands. It was the most thoughtful gift anyone had ever given her.

"*Danki,*"she said softly.

Noah looked into her eyes and the sparkle that reflected more than just the moonlight. She had such a natural beauty to her that showed humility. He was sure he wasn't meant to see beyond the tough exterior she tried very hard to keep up, but he could see her meek spirit in the reflection of her eyes. It drew him to her like a moth to a flame, burning brighter the closer he came. He wanted to draw her into his arms and kiss her soft cheek the way he had a few nights before, but he was sure she would reject such an advance. After all, she still hadn't told him her name, which showed him she didn't trust him.

Rose walked to the end of the dock to retrieve the Mason jar so she could collect enough fireflies to make a small beacon for her safe return to the dock at the conclusion of her nightly boat ride.

Noah sat in the grass on the embankment watching Rose chasing after the fireflies. He couldn't help but chuckle at her frustration when she leapt for a handful, only to come up empty-handed. In a span of several minutes, she had only caught two.

"How did you ever manage to catch an entire jar-full chasing after them like that?"

Noah's question surprised her.

"It takes a while to get a full jar. It takes patience."

Noah chuckled. "Or it requires a different method. When you chase them, it makes them scatter and fly away from you. It's almost as though they're taunting you."

Rose bristled. How did this *mann* manage to get under her skin so quickly and efficiently. It was almost as though he delighted in aggravating her.

"If you think you can do better, I challenge you to see how many you can get. They are very fast, and hard to catch."

Noah stood up, a smile slowly curving up the corners of his mouth. Rose felt herself momentarily mesmerized by his mouth, but quickly cast her eyes to the ground, grateful it was dark enough he could not see the blush that she could feel heating her cheeks.

"Pick up the jar and have it ready for me," he demanded.

Rose picked up the jar from the grass and held it out to him with fake enthusiasm, mocking him.

Noah ignored her as he planted his feet firmly in the grass and held out his hands. The fireflies swarmed around him, seemingly surrendering themselves to his open hands that he quickly cupped around them. He reached over and deposited his first handful into the jar, leaving Rose feeling like a *dummkopf* for doubting him.

Handful after handful went into the jar until he was satisfied there were enough to light her way properly. She looked at him, almost no expression on her face, that it was hard for him to detect the admiration in her eyes—but it was there.

"The trick is to let them come to you. When you chase them, they scatter, but when you stand still, they float right by you."

Rose smiled, taking the jar from him after he twisted the ring around the rim, his square of cheesecloth covering the opening. She walked slowly up the dock, Noah on her heels. She set the jar of fireflies down at the end of the dock and stepped into the boat. Noah stayed on the dock, but she could see in his eyes that he had no intention of asking to ride along with her. She could see sudden sorrow in his eyes, but beyond that, a little bit of fear.

Noah untied the rope as she slipped on her life-vest. As before, he pushed her off from shore with his foot and she began to pedal backward until she was clear from the edge of the dock. Before she left him, she looked into his face once more. He was so handsome and so vulnerable she wanted to hug him, but she knew such an advance was unacceptable. She turned the rudder and set her feet in forward motion.

"My name is Rose."

Chapter 12

Noah's heart fluttered as he watched Rose pedal away from the dock. Knowing her name seemed like such a simple gesture, but to him, it meant that she trusted him—even if only a small measure. He lowered himself onto the end of the dock intending to wait for her to return. Would she be happy to see him when came back, or would it annoy her that he was still here? Torn between what to do, he began to pray.

Gott, breathe life back into me. I want to live for you again. Forgive me for turning my back on you and my familye. Bless me with the return of my faith. And bless me with enough courage to face my familye and Emma's familye.

Noah looked out onto the water with a renewed sense of peace that could only come from *Gott*. He let his toes dip into the cool water as he listened to the gentle lapping of water against the underside of the dock. Looking up across the pond, he could see that Rose was already on her way back. Was there a reason she only went to one end and then back? Was it possible that she was still frightened from the near-drowning she experienced?

Gott, please bless Rose with peace and courage.

The prayer surprised him. It was the third time he'd prayed on her behalf. He was beginning to like the feeling of unselfishness that praying for others brought him. He had to admit that it was a little strange for him to be praying for another woman who wasn't his betrothed, but Emma was gone, and Rose was here and very much in need of prayer.

As Rose neared the dock, his heart began to flutter again. It was a feeling he hadn't felt in so long, he knew it was one to be treasured. He stood up and took the rope, tying it around the post without saying a word to her. Then he held out his hand to assist her out of the boat, and surprisingly, she took it. Her hand was warm, and fit his perfectly—so perfect he didn't want to let it go, but he did for the sake of not causing her any reason to worry about his intentions for her.

Truth be told, he was attracted to her beauty and humility, but he would not risk saying that to her. The fact that the feelings were still a little foreign to him weighed on his mind, but he tried not to let it show on his face.

"*Danki,*" she said as he released her hand. "I wasn't certain you would still be here when I finished my trip across the pond. I pray that after I do that a few more times I will be able to put the fear of drowning behind me for *gut.*"

Noah stood beside her on the dock. He was so close he could smell the sunshine that still lingered on her. "I prayed that *Gott* would give you peace and courage about what happened."

Rose's heart felt like it skipped a beat. The thought of a *mann* praying for her in such a way was a blessing in itself.

"*Danki,*" she whispered.

She continued to stand close to him, her breathing coming out in intermittent wisps. Noah could feel the heaving of his own chest in anticipation of having her closer still. She looked up at him with dreamy eyes that begged him to pull her into his arms. He wanted to respond. To hold her like it would be the last time he would ever see her.

Crickets sang loudly in the grass nearby, and fireflies fluttered and glowed magically around them. He watched her as she tipped back the *kapp* from her head and pulled the pins from her dark blond hair. She didn't take her eyes off him as she tucked the pins in her apron pocket. He couldn't resist her any longer; the pull was too strong.

Noah closed the space between him and Rose, pulling her into his arms with the sort of desperation one would expect from a heart-wrenching farewell. Then he scooped her loose hair into his fists, using it to draw her head upward. His lips touched hers and she responded with a hunger for him and the love he would give her.

Then it hit him.

He didn't know her well enough to love her.

Did he?

Was he so selfish still that he would engage her in a kiss so filled with passion, but lacking in the love it needed to back it up?

He let go of her, gazing into her eyes that were filled with hope. "I'm sorry. I shouldn't have done that. Please forgive me."

He didn't wait for a response. He left her side before he lost his nerve to do the right thing.

Chapter 13

"Noah, don't go," she begged him.

It was too late. He disappeared quickly into the darkness of the night, leaving Rose all alone. Now she understood what Katie had meant when she had told her that *menner* can be complicated. Why had Noah suddenly run off? Why had he apologized for kissing her? It was a beautiful kiss—her first.

Could it be that he wasn't ready to kiss me or any woman? Did it frighten him to let his guard down with me?

Please, Gott, if it be your wille, please let Noah love me.

Rose reached down and opened the lid to the Mason jar, letting the fireflies escape into the darkness. They glowed happily as they flitted about lighting her path to the base of the dock. Dragging her bare feet in the soft grass along the perimeter of the pond, Rose directed her reluctant steps toward the small *haus* she shared with Katie. She resisted the urge to cry, even though she really wanted to. Kissing Noah had been like a dream-come-true, and her lips still tingled from it.

ಬಂಛ

Noah called out to *Gott* as he hurried to get home. He had made a big mistake in judgment when he kissed Rose, and he had no idea how to fix it. He'd acted selfishly without any regard to her feelings.

She'd kissed him back. Hadn't she?

He hadn't been able to resist her once she pulled her hair down. Had she done that for him, or because she was uncomfortable? He'd remembered Emma telling him on many occasions how uncomfortable the head dressing could be, especially in the heat of summer. She'd enjoyed letting the breeze float through her hair many times when they were together. After all, they were to be married, and she showed her hair to him as a gift.

Had Rose offered herself to him for marriage? Panic filled him as he thought about marrying a woman other than Emma. Was he ready to consider such a thing? Was it possible she was falling for him only because he rescued her? He'd heard that those things can happen, and he needed to be sure of her feelings. Before that, he needed to keep his distance from her long enough to figure out why he'd acted so impulsively toward her.

ಬಂಛ

Rose was glad she had the day off from the B&B. She knew Bess had probably seen the kiss exchanged between her and Noah the night before, and she wasn't up for discussing it with the woman. She knew Bess meant well, only having her best interest in mind, but she would probably offer her some unwanted advice on the matter, and Rose was in no mood for it.

After breakfast, Katie rode into town with Caleb for a few supplies, promising to pick up the material for their dresses. Rose was happy for the time alone, giving her word to her *schweschder* that she would have the celery patch weeded by the time she got back. As she waved to Katie, she felt a sense of relief at having gotten through the morning meal without having to engage in anything other than talk of the wedding. Thankfully, her *schweschder* was too preoccupied to notice anything different about Rose. The fact remained she *had* changed. The kiss from Noah had changed her in a way she didn't quite understand, but she knew she couldn't wait to see him again.

Rose dragged the garden tools from the barn and headed toward Katie's celery patch which ran alongside of the large kitchen garden. She picked a ripe tomato off the vine and rubbed it on her apron to remove any dirt. As she bit into the sun-warmed fruit her gaze drifted across the pond toward Noah's *haus*. Spotting Noah on a ladder adjusting one of the crooked shutters, she wished she could see him better.

As she stared with a hand over her eyes to shield them from the bright sun, it appeared that Noah was working only in a pair of trousers.

What I wouldn't give to get my hands on those binoculars that Bess uses to keep an eye on us.

Rose giggled at her own thoughts as she reluctantly turned around to till up the rows with the garden hoe. The sun was already burning the back of her neck, and she wished she had put on her bigger bonnet. With her hands already dirty, she decided to wait until she took a water break. She intended to get two rows finished and out of the way before taking a break, but the humidity level was almost unbearable. Turning around for a brief moment to check on Noah, she was sad to see he was no longer in her line of vision. Thankfully his *haus* rested on the bank of the narrow end of the pond so it wasn't too far for her to see him if he should get back on the ladder he'd left against the side of *haus*.

Before moving onto the next row, Rose looked up again in the direction of Noah's *haus* and spotted him watching her. She waved at him, but he looked away and went back to work. Had he seen her and ignored her? She hoped it was only that he hadn't seen her wave, instead of what she feared—that he'd changed his mind about her. If he no longer wanted anything to do with her after kissing her the way he had, then she would be glad to be rid of a *mann* who would take advantage like that. On the other hand, he'd given her a beautiful kiss that she wouldn't soon forget.

Chapter 14

Rose took her time catching fireflies the way Noah had shown her the night before. She was surprised when he wasn't waiting for her at the dock the way he had for the past few nights. She hoped that if she took her time gathering fireflies, he would soon show up. But she was getting tired, and he still had not arrived. Tears stung the back of her eyes at the thought that he could be so inconsiderate.

I should have known it was too gut to be true. A mann like that would never fall in love with a woman like me. I'm too plain, and he's very handsome, ain't it so?

Suddenly, she didn't feel like going for a boat ride. She lowered herself to the end of the dock and looked at the fireflies glowing in the Mason jar. Noah had been right about them lasting longer with the cheese cloth at the top of the jar to let in air. But she was guessing he'd thought it wrong to kiss her, and that's why he wasn't here to greet her at the pond tonight.

I was right about him ignoring me when I waved to him. Why would he kiss me if he didn't like me? Does he think it too soon to fall in love again after losing his betrothed? If he did, then he should have never kissed me. Shame on him.

Rose fought the tears that stung the backs of her eyes. She swallowed hard the pain of rejection as she released the fireflies from their temporary captivity. Sadness consumed her as she stood up from the dock to find she was still alone. She knew Bess would probably have something to say about it when she arrived at work in the morning, and was not looking forward to it.

ಬಆ

Several times Noah set out to meet Rose at the dock at the B&B, but every time, his feet would not take him past his own yard. It wasn't that he didn't care for her—he did, and that's what scared him so much. He just wasn't ready to face her until he had sorted out the end to his grieving. He needed to end the mourning period, but he just didn't know how to let go of something he'd held onto for so long—even if he *was* ready. It wasn't fair to Rose if he were to move forward with her when he hadn't yet closed the door on his past. He knew the only way to close that door was to face her *familye* and his own once and for all.

Having not spoken to anyone since Emma's funeral, he worried that they would reject him. He also worried he may have been shunned, and figured a visit to Bishop Troyer would be his first order of business. He intended to pursue his interest in Rose so he could get to know her better, but there were a few things he had to take care of first. He prayed she would understand, and not form a low opinion of him because of his actions.

ഇരു

"If there's one thing I do know about *menner,* they get spooked easily like horses," Bess said as she helped Rose set out the place settings at the dining room table. "If you ask me, I think he's feeling guilty for kissing you."

Rose sucked in her bottom lip. "Because of Emma?"

"*Jah,* but don't worry. Noah is an honorable *mann.* He wouldn't kiss you unless he really liked you. He just needs some time to sort out his feelings."

Rose's heart quickened at the thought of Noah liking her.

"I have to say something else to you. I noticed you took your hair down from your prayer *kapp.*"

Rose couldn't look Bess in the eye. "I have seen Katie do the same for Caleb. I only wanted Noah to think I was pretty like my *schweschder.*"

Bess placed cutlery at each place setting. "That sort of thing will make a *mann* think you are interested in marriage."

Rose smiled. "*Jah,* that's why I did it. To see if he would receive me. I thought he had, but now I can't be certain. His absence from the pond last night has made me worry I acted in haste."

Bess smiled knowingly. "Love always makes people act in haste. There is no way around it. But it is worth it if you can work through all the ups and downs of relationships. They take a lot of work."

Rose looked at Bess shyly. "I wouldn't say that Noah and I have a relationship."

Bess put down the linens she was folding into swan-shaped napkins. "*Jah,* you do. Even if it's only a friendship. You have a relationship with him now, a bond that cannot be broken."

"But he's already broken it." Rose collapsed into one of the dining room chairs.

Bess crossed the room and sat across from Rose. "It's not broken. It's just getting started. And new relationships can take the most time. So much time, in fact, that it might seem that they're moving backward, but I assure you it's not broken."

"How can you be sure?"

"He just needs some time to digest it like a heavy meal. That kiss might have come a little too soon, but it did happen. It happened because he obviously is interested in you. A *mann* doesn't kiss a woman like that if isn't interested in her becoming part of his future."

Rose blushed at her comments.

"Noah has lost at love once already, and he is probably afraid he could lose you too. Loving another can be scary. There is always risk in loving someone, but the risk is always worth it. When he realizes that, he will come back around."

Rose hoped Bess was right about Noah and his potential interest in her. If she wasn't, Rose wasn't sure she could survive such a heartbreak.

Chapter 15

Noah stood in front of the small mirror at the bathroom sink for some time, staring at his reflection. Even with the scissors in hand, he found it difficult to part with his shoulder-length hair. He hadn't cut it since Emma had died. In some ways, it was a symbol of his loss—his outward sign of mourning. Was he truly ready to put it behind him and let go of Emma forever?

An image of Rose entered his mind. Her natural beauty and humbleness pulled him toward her like a magnetic force. He had thought he would never be able to love again, but here he was, feeling very strongly for Rose, and he couldn't ignore it much longer. He wanted to know everything about her. He wanted to catch fireflies with her and hold her in his arms.

But he couldn't.

Not yet.

First, he had to cut his hair and his ties to Emma. Then he would go to see the Bishop. Rose would certainly be more eager to accept him if he made his commitment to the community and the church known. Was he already considering marriage with Rose? How could he not? She was the angel who had pulled him from the darkness that was his life until only a few days ago.

Noah lifted the scissors to his hair and snipped the first piece. Regulation stated that he was to have his bangs trimmed straight across. He'd never really liked the look, to be truthful, but his long hair would not go over well with the community or the Bishop. If he wanted to remain and have a chance to pursue Rose he must cut it straight across.

Noah sighed as he snipped another chunk from the front of his hair. He had been in a state of rebellion against the community for so long that suddenly he questioned the rules he had adhered to his entire life.

It was only hair.

Was it really that important?

The humble style established conformity, and that was important within the community. But that didn't mean Noah liked the look. Such thoughts would be considered prideful, but he'd seen the admiration in Rose's eyes when she looked at his hair. He'd felt her fingers glide through it when he'd kissed her. Shivers ran through him at the thought of having Rose's fingers tangled up in his hair.

It didn't matter that he wanted to keep his hair.

Cut it, he must.

It was the only way to remain in the community.

Snipping the last section in the front, Noah had set the precedent for rest of the hair to go. But as he did, he realized it was no longer Emma that he clung to; it was Rose and her fingers playing delightfully in his long hair.

Another few snips to the sides, and he was almost there. He could feel the rebellion leaving him with each snip. And as the hair fell to the floor, so did his ties with Emma. Through his prayers, Noah had resolved that Emma was not meant to stay with him; she was destined to be with *Gott.*

This would be a new start, and his hair was still long enough that Rose could run her fingers through it freely. Did he want her to? The answer was a resounding *yes.*

Unable to see the back, Noah wasn't certain if he'd managed to cut a straight line, but it was now short enough that the imperfections would be hidden beneath his hat.

Next, he would tackle the scruff of whiskers that he'd kept trimmed in more of an *Englisch* style. After rinsing the bone-handled shaving brush, he swished the horse-hair bristles against the cake of peppermint soap at the bottom of the old *kaffi* cup he kept it in. Thick, soapy lather formed on the end of the brush, and he lifted it to the chiseled angle of his jaw. The cooling soap spread smoothly across his face, creating a white beard.

He paused for a minute, thinking it funny that he could one day have a white beard, but not until after he and Rose had had a full life together. No matter what, he couldn't keep his mind off her. It seemed that every plan that came to his mind lately involved her somehow. One question weighed on his mind though; was she thinking the same things?

Lifting the straight razor that he'd sharpened on the leather strap, he scraped it across his chin carefully. He was careful to take small strokes and rinse the blade after each stroke to avoid cutting himself. The whiskers were tough, and would require a second pass with the blade, but slow progress was changing his look in ways he was no longer used to.

Would Rose like his new look? Most women, it seemed, preferred the clean-shaven look. But he had also noticed admiration in Rose's eyes every time he rubbed his chin in her presence. Her eyes had followed his hand as he'd swiped it across his whiskers; it had not gone unnoticed.

With the majority of his whiskers now gone, Noah rinsed his face and began the process all over again, this time pulling the blade a little tighter against his skin. His skin felt bare and vulnerable the way it always did after a clean shave. A final rinse of his face and shaving supplies, and Noah was finally done.

He stood there for a moment, examining his new look, and feeling unsure about it. He hoped Rose would approve of his new look since she'd not met him looking this way.

Certainly now he would be presentable to the Bishop and the community, and that was what he wanted.

Chapter 16

Rose dragged the hose over to the celery patch so she could set the sprinkler on it. The soil was getting dry, and she didn't want the plants she'd been entrusted with to wilt in the hot sun. She'd made sure that the gas-powered generator in the shed was running so it would power the sump-pump to bring water up from the well. Everything at her parent's *haus* was a little easier since it was all solar-powered, but *Aenti* Nettie's small farm was still surviving on more primitive means.

She stood watching the track of the sprinkler to make sure it was reaching all the way to the end of the celery patch. When she was satisfied every last stalk was getting its fill of water, she turned to leave. She'd purposely kept her back to the pond; the temptation to look for Noah was too great. It had been three long days since their kiss, and she'd sat at the end of the dock each night waiting for him, only to return home each night disappointed. Not only had he not shown up to meet her, there was no indication he'd even been there since the night they'd kissed. He'd also made no attempt to see her in any way, and that had instilled deep feelings of discouragement in her.

A faint splash from behind her forced her gaze toward the pond, where Noah stood on the other side skipping a rock across half the expanse. Was he trying to get her attention?

He certainly had it now.

She couldn't resist watching as he tossed another. Her gaze followed the stone as it skipped across the surface five times before sinking. Looking up from the pond, Noah made eye contact with her even from that distance. He stood there for a few moments, staring across the water at her, and then removed his hat and held it in his hands. Rose nearly gasped as her hand instinctively clamped across her mouth.

He's gone and cut his hair. And he shaved too!

Rose remembered the feel of his long, silky hair entwined in her fingers the night the two of them kissed. The tickle of his whiskers had given her goose-flesh when his lips had swept over hers. What would a kiss be like with him now? Would she ever get the chance to see?

From across the pond, Noah lifted his hat in a salutatory wave before placing it back on his head. Then he turned and walked toward his *haus* without looking back.

Rose's heart thumped against her ribcage. He'd waved—sort of. It wasn't much, but it was something.

She wished she knew what was going on with him, but he had cut his hair and shaved his face clean. Though he now looked *Amish,* Rose would not soon forget the sultry look in Noah that had attracted her to him in the first place. At least now, with the changes he'd made, she felt confident that she had a chance to have a life with him in the community. Unless it was too late, and he'd already been shunned.

Please, Gott, allow Noah to remain in the community. I think I've fallen in leib with him. Please, Gott, make it so.

Rose couldn't wait to get to work so she could discuss Noah's changes with Bess. Katie would never understand such a dilemma, and if she confided in her, she ran the risk that Caleb would discover his cousin was living there. Noah had warned her that he wanted his presence kept secret, but she hoped his change in appearance meant he had changed his mind. Was it too much to hope that he was getting himself ready to rejoin the community? She certainly hoped it was so.

ঙ৩৫

Noah hitched up his buggy as he rehearsed what he planned on saying to the Bishop. He disliked showing up unannounced, but he hadn't been to church services in so long, there wasn't a chance to prearrange a meeting with him. He was nervous, that was for certain, but he knew if he let it show, it would put him at a disadvantage with the Bishop. Bishop Troyer encouraged confidence among the *menner* in the community. At the moment, Noah could only feel numbness mixed with a bit of apprehension. His prayers had left him confident that he was doing the right thing—that he was finally ready to move forward out of his mourning period and get on with his life. He hoped it wasn't too late to be welcomed back into the community where he knew he belonged.

As he pulled his buggy in front of the Bishop's *haus,* Noah was confident that he would have the right words to make things right for his return to the community.

Bishop Troyer stepped out of his barn at the sound of an approaching buggy. He tipped his hat forward to shield his eyes from the sun so he could see who had come to visit. His heart leapt for joy when he saw that it was Noah Beiler. He quickened his steps to greet the young *mann,* who had fallen away from his flock too long ago.

Noah stepped out of the buggy, still feeling a little unsure of himself, until he saw the look in Bishop Troyer's eyes as he approached him. The older *mann* threw his arms around him, welcoming him, making Noah's apprehension slip away.

"Noah, it's so *gut* to see you. I've prayed that *Gott* would bring you back to us, and here you are. *Kume,* we will go inside and see if there is any lemonade left. I could use a refreshing drink on such a warm day as this."

Noah followed Bishop Troyer into the *haus,* thinking that a sip of *Fraa* Troyer's tart lemonade was just what he needed.

Chapter 17

Rose fidgeted on the backless bench during church service. It was too warm to sit there for so long, and her legs and back ached from working so much in the celery patch and the B&B over the last week. She was not looking forward to wash-day tomorrow, as she would be doing her own wash as well as all the linens for the B&B. The best thing about her job was having Bess to confide her worries to over Noah.

Since the *menner* sat on one side of the room, she was stuck sitting next to Katie, who wasn't paying any more attention to the service than she was. The big difference between she and Katie, was that her *schweschder* was confident of her relationship with the *mann* who sat across the row from where they were. Caleb was making sheep-eyes at his betrothed when he thought Rose was not looking. Noah, who was at the front of the large room, sat wedged between two of the Elders, as though they guarded him.

With the windows open, the aroma of honeysuckle blooms floated in on the warm breeze. Rose took a deep breath of the sweet flowery air as it wafted by her. It reminded her of the night she and Noah had shared their one and only kiss. She had smelled the flowers that warm evening from the bushes that grew to each side of the dock at the B&B. The aroma had contributed to the romantic feel of the night, and Rose couldn't let go of that feeling—even now.

Katie nudged her in the arm. "Get up, Rose, the service is over."

Rose blinked.

The room was emptying of the community, and she was the only one still sitting. Feeling her cheeks heat up, she had to wonder how long she'd been sitting there staring unresponsively. Had Noah seen her when he'd walked past her?

"What's wrong with you, Rose?" Katie asked impatiently.

"I...I was reflecting on some things," Rose stammered. It wasn't a lie, but it also wasn't the sort of thing she should have been thinking about during church.

Pushing down embarrassment, Rose stood and followed Katie into the kitchen where most of the women had gathered. Most of the *menner* had already gathered in the yard with the *kinner,* except for the few that had already begun to take the benches outside for the meal. Rose glanced out the kitchen window and spotted Noah helping Caleb and a few others set up tables in a long line under the shade of the many trees.

She paused to admire the smile that played along his lips every time one of the *menner* spoke to him. He seemed genuinely happy to be back in the community, and the *menner* had obviously welcomed him back—except for one, who seemed to keep his distance. She watched the strain crease Noah's brow as the older *mann* approached him.

ৼৄৡ

Noah felt his chest tighten as Emma's *vadder* approached him in the yard after church. He'd both dreaded this moment and eagerly anticipated it ever since his meeting with Bishop Troyer. Greeting him with apprehension, Noah took a deep breath and tried to remember the words of wisdom the Bishop had shared with him.

"Abraham, it's *gut* to see you. You and Mary look well. I've missed you both very much." Noah stammered over his words hoping they would be well-received, but he couldn't be sure from the older *mann's* expression.

Abraham paused. "Mary and I have been concerned for you, Noah. How long have you been back in the community?"

Noah felt his heart thump against his ribcage.

"I've been here all along. I never left. I'm sorry for not coming to see you sooner, but I just couldn't bring myself to face the two of you."

Abraham placed a hand on Noah's shoulder.

"You were like a son to us. That hasn't changed. We know you did everything you could to save our Emma, including diving into the icy pond to pull her out. She is with *Gott,* and remaining closed off from your *familye* would not have brought her back to us."

"I know that now that I've spent the past year and a half rejecting the community. It means a lot to me that you and Mary are so willing to accept me now that I'm back."

Abraham swallowed the sorrow that formed in his throat. "We love you like one of our own. We want you to be happy and to feel free to move on with your life. You're too young to be alone. You deserve to find a *fraa* and have *kinner."*

Noah was happy to hear Abraham's words, but he wondered if he would still feel the same if he knew he'd already developed strong feelings for Rose. The very thought of her sent delightful shivers through him. He only hoped that his delay in seeing her hadn't ruined his chances with her. But he was still not done putting his life back in order.

His own *vadder* still hadn't received him, and he worried that if he took too long to mend fences with him it could hinder the relationship he desired with Rose. Even though his *daed* and Rose each stood only a few feet from him, he could not go to either of them. His *daed* needed time, and Rose was just out of his reach because of his unsettled life. He would not hurt her more than he may already have.

Rose set a casserole dish on the table in front of Noah. He didn't smell the food; he only smelled honeysuckle, even if just from memory of the night they'd shared such a beautiful kiss. How would he be able to bear it if he had to continue to put a life with her on hold until he set things right with his *daed?*

Was it possible for him to do both?

Chapter 18

Rose lingered at the table near Noah, hoping he would speak to her, but so far he hadn't. There was only so much rearranging of the stacks of plates left on the table that she could do near him without making herself look desperate for his attention. When she'd finished laying out all the place settings available, she slammed the last plate against the table hard enough to break it. Still, he did not acknowledge her. Was it possible he regretted kissing her? Perhaps it was a moment of weakness on his part, and he wished to take it back.

Choking down tears, Rose turned her back to him and walked out toward the edge of the property. She didn't want to be anywhere near him if he didn't like her. She'd prayed that the kiss had meant as much to him as it had to her, but now she wasn't so sure it had ever happened. At the time, she'd been stressed and emotional from nearly drowning. Was it possible she'd imagined the whole thing? His appearance now made her wonder if he had rejoined the community with another woman on his mind—a woman who was not her.

Rose collapsed at the base of a large oak tree. Who was she kidding? Noah was very handsome and could have his choice of any woman in the community. Why would he choose her? She was far too plain and had nothing to offer him.

ഇൗരു

Noah couldn't help but follow Rose, who was obviously upset from his lack of acknowledgment of her. He wasn't trying to ignore her, but it was obvious she saw it that way. The last thing he wanted to do was hurt her. But no matter how hard he'd tried to spare her feelings, he'd managed to do the exact opposite. Now he would have to explain things to her, when he'd hoped he would be able to avoid this conversation with her.

He slowly approached the tree and leaned against it. "There's a nice breeze under this tree. I can see why you picked this spot. It's kind of crowded over there with the entire community trying to eat all at once."

Startled by his presence, Rose bit back the tears that threatened to spill from her eyes, and looked off into the distance. She allowed the rustling of the leaves to soothe her as she calmed herself enough to speak.

"Why are you following me? Don't you have other interests to pursue?"

Noah was baffled by her question. "*Mei daed* won't speak to me for not telling him where I was all this time."

Rose looked up into his blue eyes. "I'm sorry that your *daed* has shunned you. But what does that have to do with me?"

Noah kicked at acorns in the grass trying to quell his nervousness. "It doesn't, but I was hoping I could bend your ear a little. I thought we were friends."

Rose cringed at the word.

Friends.

So that was all she was to him? He'd made it clear by saying the word. She didn't want to be his friend. She wanted more from him than that. If all he wanted was friendship, she didn't think she could handle that—especially if he should decide to begin dating someone else. But he'd said it, and there was no ignoring it.

If he wants to be friends, I will be the best friend he's ever had. Gott, please let him see me as more than a friend.

"*Jah,* I suppose we are...*friends.*"

The word didn't come out as gracefully as she was trying for, and Noah noticed her strange tone.

Noah cleared his throat, feeling suddenly awkward with the silence between them. "Would you like to come back to the meal with me? I'm sure everyone is seated and eating by now."

Noah wished he could sit with her, but the rules stated they were to sit at opposite sides of the table. There were some rules he didn't agree with even though he'd followed them all his life. He'd wanted to sit with her during church service as well, but that was also not allowed.

"I'm not real hungry. I'd rather go home. I woke up with a headache, and it doesn't want to go away."

Noah kicked at the acorns nervously. "I rode with Caleb this morning, or I'd offer you a ride."

"I don't mind walking. It's not that far. I can't take our buggy or Katie will have to walk home, and she will have dishes to bring back with her."

"Would you mind if I walked with you? I don't really want to hang around there anymore with my *daed's* disapproving looks."

Rose took the hand Noah offered, stood up and dusted off the back of her dress. "You have to face him eventually."

They began to walk toward Goose pond where they both lived.

Noah sighed. "I tried to talk to him, but he doesn't understand. He thinks I turned my back on my *familye* and the community."

Rose looked at him as they walked slowly along the road. "I can see how he might think that. You said yourself that you were dead to them."

"Jah, I did, and I was wrong. I've spent a lot of time in prayer lately, and *Gott* has shown me that leaving the community and turning my back on my

faith was the worst thing I could have done to help myself heal from what happened. I have to find a way to get *mei daed* to see that I'm truly repentant."

"Perhaps your constant presence in the community from here on out will let him see you are serious about your commitment, and he will accept it with time."

"He hasn't ever really approved of me. He always said I had a rebellious streak in me. I'm certain he is correct since I don't like some of the rules we live by."

Rose had always felt the same way, but had never dared voice the opinion to anyone. "My *familye* refers to me as *independent,* but what they really mean is rebellious. I am the same way."

Noah smiled as he slipped his hand in hers, swinging her arm slightly as they walked along; the hot sun heating their backsides.

Chapter 19

By the time they reached her *aenti* Nettie's small farmhouse, Rose had a better understanding of what Noah had gone through after Emma's death. She knew it was best to be a friend to Noah, and be patient about the rest of it. She feared that if she pressed him for more he may withdraw even further from her, and he was finally talking to her again.

Noah walked her to the back door. He wanted to pull her into his arms and hold her. He'd missed her this past week that he'd been busy working on his return to the community. But the truth was, he didn't trust himself not to get too caught up in her, and that wouldn't be fair to her as long as he still had personal issues to work out. Instead, he reached up and placed a kiss on her forehead, hoping it would convey his feelings to her without going overboard. She responded with a sigh, and he hoped that meant she understood his position.

Noah stepped away from her and turned to leave. He waved over his shoulder while she stood there with a stunned look on her face. He didn't want to leave her, but he had to—for both their sakes.

Rose felt her heartbeat catch in her chest as his lips touched her forehead. She was sure he would give her more than that, but to her disappointment, he hadn't. She took that as his way of letting her know that they were indeed friends, and nothing more. When he'd held her hand as he walked her home, she'd hoped that it meant something, but it was obvious it didn't. How was she supposed to go from a kiss as passionate as they had shared to accepting kisses on her forehead? As she watched him walk away, she felt like a *dummkopf* for thinking he could ever be interested in her for more than friendship.

ഇൽ

Rose stretched on her tiptoes to reach the clothesline at the B&B so she could help Bess hang the bed linens they had washed. Her last load of personal wash was still hanging on the line at home, where it would be waiting for her after she finished work for the day. It was only three o'clock, and she was already exhausted. She'd tossed about most of the night worrying about Noah, even though she knew worrying would not change the situation.

Bess pinned the other end of the queen-size sheet to the clothesline. "Are you going to tell me what happened when Noah walked you home yesterday, or do I have to pull it out of you?"

Rose sighed with frustration. "There isn't anything to tell."

"I saw the two of you holding hands as you walked down the road. That's something."

Rose's heart skipped a beat. "Did anyone else see?"

Bess picked up a pillow slip and pinned it to the line. "*Nee,* everyone had bowed their head for the prayer. By the time they lifted their heads, you were long down the road out of sight. Is that all you have to say about that?"

"There isn't anything to tell. He only wants to be friends. He said so."

Bess flashed her one of her unconvincing, crooked smiles. "Seems to me, a *mann* doesn't hold a woman's hand unless he likes her for more than friendship."

"That was my way of thinking too, but then he kissed me on the forehead before he left. And he actually asked if we were friends. All he wants is friendship."

Bess stopped what she was doing and peeked at Rose from behind the hanging linens. "And you want more than friendship?"

"*Jah.*"

Bess walked around between the laundry to face her. "Then you have to show him what it would be like to have more than that."

Rose sighed again. "How am I supposed to do that?"

Bess smiled. "For starters, you need to give him an opportunity to miss you, and then you surprise him by doing something he wouldn't expect."

Rose was already feeling overwhelmed. "What do you mean?"

"Don't go to the dock tonight. He expects that, and if you're not there, he will have the chance to miss you."

Rose hung up the last pillow slip. "He hasn't met me there all week, so that won't work."

Bess laughed. "Just because he didn't meet you doesn't mean he didn't know you were there. I saw him watching you. I could tell it was tearing him up not to meet you. But if you're not there, it will make him wonder why."

Rose couldn't believe what Bess was saying. Was it possible that he was still interested in her?

"What is it that I can do that he won't expect? Or was that it?"

Bess tried not to smile. "Ever since the accident with Emma, I've taken food over to Noah once a week and left it on his doorstep. I'm pretty sure he knew it was me, but he never came out of the *haus* until after I left. What if you took him a basket of food in the morning instead of me taking it?"

Rose picked up the laundry hamper and walked toward the back door with it. "That doesn't sound like much."

"My point is, Rose, that Noah won't expect *you* to be delivering him a food basket. I haven't even dropped one off in two weeks, so he won't be expecting it at all. But when he sees that you have done this for him, it will soften his heart toward you, and might afford you the opportunity to talk to him."

It all sounded too simple, but Rose was willing to give it a try if it meant she would have the chance to see Noah again. Truth be told, she wasn't too keen on the idea of skipping her trip to the dock tonight, but she was of the mindset that she had nothing more to lose.

Chapter 20

Rose woke earlier than usual so she would have enough time to get over to the B&B to get the food basket from Bess so she could get it to Noah before he went about his day. She'd practically had to sit on her hands the night before so she wouldn't be tempted to go to the dock with the hope of seeing Noah. She hoped Bess's plan would work and Noah had noticed she wasn't there and had missed her. She supposed she would find out soon enough.

As she pulled on a clean, purple dress, Rose eyed the attending dress she had worked on last night while Katie and Caleb sat on the porch swing talking of wedding plans. She was glad in a way that she'd stayed home to work on the dress, especially since she had made a lot of progress. Katie had already inquired why there wasn't much done on the dress yet, and now she would be able to present her *schweschder* with a nearly finished product.

Rose tip-toed out of the *haus* so she wouldn't disturb Katie. She wasn't up for any questions about what she was doing or where she was going. She was a little nervous about Bess's plan, but figured it might be the only way she could appeal to Noah's heart.

When she arrived at the B&B, Bess had the basket already prepared. She'd packed it with half a dozen fresh eggs, a loaf of freshly-baked bread, cinnamon rolls, a bag of oats, a small bag of ground *kaffi,* a small bowl of freshly-picked strawberries, and a Mason jar filled with milk fresh from the morning milking. The basket was rather heavy, but Rose was determined to set out on foot to deliver it, despite Bess's offer to use her buggy. It didn't make sense when she could be half-way there in the time it would take to hitch up the buggy. Little did she know that she would end up feeling differently by the time she reached Noah's doorstep. Sweat rolled down her back beneath her dress, but thankfully, the slight breeze had kept her face dry.

Rose hefted the large basket from her hip, where she'd rested it like a *boppli,* and set it on the porch step at the back of the *haus.* She admired the fresh coat of paint on the clapboard siding and the neatness of the porch. A wooden, folding chair sat in the corner near the rail, and a galvanized watering can contained freshly-picked hydrangeas in a variety of hues. It seemed like an odd thing to see on the porch of a *mann's haus,* but she already knew him to be a sensitive, creative type. The yard had been cleared of debris and thick weeds to the point of resembling a roughly-cut lawn. It was apparent that Noah had been hard at work trying to resurrect his small farm *haus* to the point Rose thought it was beginning to look like a home.

She turned to leave, her thoughts of what it would be like to live in the small *haus* with Noah interrupted when the back door swung open.

"Won't you stay and join me for a little breakfast?"

Noah's deep voice caught Rose by surprise. She turned and searched his face for sincerity. Finding it, she smiled her answer, and then followed him into the small *haus*. It was apparent by the scant furniture and bare windows that there was still a lot of work to be done inside to make it look more like the outside, but it was still a comfortable space.

Noah offered her a chair at the small, round table in the kitchen. She wouldn't admit to him that she'd left the *haus* without her own breakfast so she could bring him the basket of food, but the aroma from the still-warm cinnamon rolls was making her mouth water. Setting two mismatched plates on the table, Noah urged her to help herself to the food she'd brought for him.

"I see *Aenti* Bess has you running her errands for her now."

All that time she'd been confiding in the older woman, and she'd not known the relationship between her and Noah. She felt her cheeks warm over embarrassment from going on like such a love-struck school-girl over Noah to his *aenti*. Why hadn't Bess told her Noah was her nephew?

"*Mei* own *vadder* won't speak to me, but *Aenti* has always been there for me. Even when I couldn't help myself."

Rose cleared her throat. "She told me that she'd been leaving baskets of food for you all this time, and when she asked me to do it for her this morning, I could hardly turn her down. But she didn't tell me she was your *aenti*."

"I'm not surprised. If I know *Aenti* Bess, she had ulterior motives for sending you over here. She probably has the notion if she throws us together we will fall in *lieb*."

Rose's heart fluttered all the way to her toes. "I haven't known her long, but I enjoy working for her. She has a *gut* heart."

Was it possible that Bess's plan was working?

Noah served her a glass of milk and a cinnamon roll. She wondered what it would be like to be the one serving him a meal in this quaint little farm *haus*. She felt terrible sitting there allowing a *mann* to serve her, but he didn't seem to mind.

"*Aenti* Bess is *mei mamm's* youngest *schweschder*. *Mei daed* always tried to keep me at a distance from her, but she was always my favorite *aenti*. *Mei daed* always said that because *Aenti* Bess was the youngest of the twelve *kinner*, that by the time she came along, her parents were too old to raise her properly and it caused her to develop a rebellious streak. I think that's why I like her so much. She's never judged me, even when I turned my back on the community. She helped me and didn't pressure me to come back until I was ready, but she was there for me in the meantime. Knowing she was there for me is what kept me from slipping completely away from everyone. With *mei mamm* gone, I feel even closer to her."

Rose hadn't realized until now just how much loss Noah had endured in his life. She was grateful that Bess really loved her nephew. She felt suddenly right about her decision to confide in her, as it was obvious she did indeed have a very *gut* heart.

Chapter 21

"Katie is NOT going to be happy when she finds out Jessup King is a guest here!"

Bess steered Rose to sit at the kitchen table and placed a glass of cool lemonade in front of her.

"That's why we will not be telling her. He is a paying guest and he has business in town. I expect you to respect the privacy of the guests here."

Rose gulped the tart lemonade. "I'm sorry, Bess. But what if Katie finds out he's in town?"

Bess sat down across from Rose and fanned her warm face with her apron. "His business with Katie is over and done with. I won't tolerate gossip about my guests."

Rose had never heard Bess talk so firmly, and she tried to understand the situation from the business side of things. But if she didn't know any better, it almost seemed that Bess was jumping to Jessup's defense. For the life of her, Rose couldn't think of a single reason other than for business that Bess would do such a thing. She knew the guest roster had slowed down a bit, but Bess had told her that was normal until July when folks usually started taking their vacations. Still, why would Bess be so defensive regarding Jessup King? From her experience in watching his relationship with her *schweschder* unfold, he had not been the kindest *mann.*

Rose looked at Bess sheepishly. "I will keep my personal feelings regarding Jessup to myself. You have been very kind to me, and I would never want to be the cause of you losing business because I couldn't control my tongue."

Bess smiled. *"Danki.* Now tell me what happened over breakfast with Noah."

The eagerness in Bess's eyes helped Rose to relax. "Why didn't you tell me he was your nephew?"

"Noah was *mei schweschder's* only *boppli.* He's pretty special to me. I really miss his *mamm.* We were the only two girls in the *familye.* It was hard to grow up with ten bruders, but *mei schweschder* and I had a special bond."

"How long ago did you lose her?"

"It's been going on five years now. Poor Noah lost his *mamm* and Emma right close to each other. It's no wonder he needed so much time to get over it."

Rose pinched her eyebrows together in a deep furrow. "Do you think he's over her?"

Bess smiled and nodded. "Over Emma? *Jah.* Noah is an honorable young *mann.* He wouldn't have kissed you if he wasn't ready to move on with his life. He's put his past behind him."

Rose didn't feel too confident of Bess's answer even though she had no reason to doubt the woman's word. Still, she worried that her accident in the pond may have forced Noah out of hiding before he was ready. Even if all signs pointed toward his recovery, she had to wonder why he still held back his feelings for her after the single kiss they'd shared.

"I hope you're right, Bess. I'm glad you made me take the food to him. He shared it with me and we had a pleasant meal together. I learned a lot more about him, but I have to wonder if he has changed his mind about me. I don't think he wants anything more than friendship."

Bess got up and brought a plate of fresh cookies to the table to go with their lemonade. "What would make you think a thing like that? Did he say he only wanted friendship?"

"Not in so many words, but *jah,* he has made it clear with his actions that he doesn't want to take our relationship beyond friendship."

Bess bit into a sugar cookie. "Maybe he's trying to slow things down. You got a kiss out of him pretty soon after you met him. He might want to get to know you—the way you did this morning at breakfast."

Rose couldn't deny that he still seemed to want her in his life, but he had distanced himself physically from her. She'd enjoyed his company this morning, but she'd hoped for a kiss when they parted, but he hadn't even attempted it. She was comfortable with taking things slow, but she worried things had come to a complete stop with Noah.

"Are you planning on going for a boat ride this evening?"

Rose thought about it for a minute. She wanted the chance to run into Noah, but she was now fearful that if he didn't show, she would feel let down.

"Do you think I should?"

Bess smiled. "I saw him skipping rocks on the pond last night. He noticed you weren't there. I think it's safe to say he missed you. So I think you should go and see if he shows up. If he doesn't, don't take it personally. He may not be ready."

Don't take it personally? How can I take it any other way if he doesn't show up to meet me?

Rose agreed to go and to give Noah some space. She knew he might need more time, and she felt he would be well worth the wait.

Chapter 22

Rose walked to the end of the dock to retrieve the Mason jar so she could catch a jar-full of fireflies. She hadn't yet seen any sign of Noah, but she was a little earlier than usual. She was so eager for the possibility of seeing him that she had practically ran out of the *haus* after the supper dishes had been done. Katie was too preoccupied with Caleb to pay her any mind, and for once, she was happy about that.

Crickets chirped and frogs croaked, bringing the humid, summer night to life. Clear skies boasted millions of stars, giving it a magical feel that Rose never got to see beyond the bright lights of the city that was too close to where she had lived before.

Fireflies danced around her, daring her to capture them. Remaining still, just as Noah had shown her, she watched their lights blink on and off in tune with the symphony playing in her head. She'd hidden her love for classical music from her *familye,* knowing it was forbidden in the Ordnung. Knowing this did not make her love for it any less. Rose hummed and twirled in the swarm of fireflies, lost in thought.

"Sounds like Mozart."

Noah's voice stopped Rose in her tracks and she looked into his smiling eyes. "You know the music of Mozart?"

"Jah, I listen to it on my battery-operated radio."

Noah couldn't help but admire her beauty. He'd caught her at a vulnerable moment, and it made her even more appealing to him. How could he possibly resist her? It wouldn't be easy, but he wouldn't rush to her either, for fear of scaring her away. Instead, he slowly closed the space between them, grabbing a handful of fireflies and pushing them into the jar she held. He took hold of the lid, placed the cheese cloth on top, and then twisted the lid in place before they could escape. All this he did without taking his eyes off Rose.

Mesmerized by her gaze, he stood close enough to her that he could hear her breath catch in her throat, his presence causing her to gasp. His heart beat in perfect tempo with the cricket's song as he leaned down and brushed a kiss against her temple. Her hair smelled like sweet strawberries ripened by warm sunshine.

"You are so beautiful," he whispered close to her ear.

Noah's warm breath sent shivers from her ear all the way to her toes. Had he called her beautiful? Such talk of vanity was forbidden, but it delighted her to hear it from his full lips that taunted her. She wanted to kiss him, but didn't dare make a move toward him, fearing he would run from her again. She remained still and allowed him to sweep kisses across her cheek until finally he reached her eager lips. Unable to hold back any longer, she deepened the kiss, reaching up and tangling her fingers in his silky hair. Oh how she'd longed for this moment. She'd dreamed of it over and over again, reliving that first kiss. But now she wouldn't have to. He was holding her close again, and unpinning her hair from her *kapp.* She delighted in the feel of his fingers in her hair as she continued to kiss him. She felt his arms tighten around her, pulling her close enough to warm her.

Noah couldn't help but pull Rose closer to him. He wanted her to be a part of him, but he had no right since she was not his *fraa*—but he wanted her to be.

"Marry me, Rose," he whispered.

Rose gasped.

He hadn't meant to say it. He'd felt it in the heat of the moment, but he knew it was too soon. But that hadn't stopped him from feeling it.

Rose stepped away from him. It was much too soon to think about marrying Noah—wasn't it? She wanted it more than anything, but she didn't really think he was ready. Was it possible he'd gotten caught up in the moment? Surely he would feel differently tomorrow, and she would be left feeling like a *dummkopf* for blurting out the answer she longed to say. She wanted to marry him more than anything, but not if he wasn't ready. They hadn't known each other long enough for that sort of thing to be anything more than a fleeting thought. The stunned look on her face sent the message to him without her having to utter a word.

Noah stepped back, allowing Rose to fall from his grasp. The moment was gone. The look on her face told him he had made a big mistake in voicing his feelings aloud. Would she be the one to run from *him* this time? Her expression let him know he'd gone too far. There was no taking it back. What could he do? Would she even take him seriously after such a foolish statement? He was falling in love with her, that much he knew for certain. He couldn't help it. *Gott* himself had placed her in his path, and he couldn't reject such a precious gift. But how could he make her understand he'd meant what he'd said without scaring her away?

"Rose, I'm sorry. I didn't mean for that to come out. I was caught up in the kiss. I feel like I keep messing things up without meaning to, and I'm sorry. I don't want to hurt you. I care about you."

There it was—his confession. He hadn't meant it at all. She'd been a fool to hope he had.

He cares about me, but he doesn't love me. How could I have allowed him to pull me into another passionate kiss without knowing how he felt about me first? I wish I could take it back. All of it. Maybe then I wouldn't feel like a dummkopf and this wouldn't hurt so much.

"I should go," she managed.

Rose couldn't face him. And she certainly couldn't come back to the pond ever again.

Chapter 23

Rose wept quietly into her pillow. She didn't want to risk having to explain her tears to Katie if she should hear her. How could she have been such a fool to let Noah use her to feed his own cravings for a replacement for Emma? Was he using her as a substitute to quench the pain of losing Emma?

Then it hit her. He'd said *her* name. He'd asked *her* to marry him. He hadn't mistakenly called her Emma like he had that first night when she'd nearly drowned. Was it possible he'd fallen in love with *her*, and he was truly over Emma?

Sitting up, Rose wiped her tear-soaked eyes on the sheet. She'd wasted what might possibly have been her only proposal of marriage, and she'd rejected him. Panic consumed her at the thought of losing Noah completely. Was it too late to tell him yes? Would he still want to marry her after the way she'd behaved?

Gott, please bless me with the strength to endure the heartache if Noah should decide he doesn't really want to marry me. I pray that he does, and that you will soften his heart toward me to forgive me for rejecting him. I didn't mean to. I love him, Gott. Please open his eyes to see the love I have for him.

ဆာ

"Where are you going in such a hurry?"

Rose gulped the last sip of her *kaffi* and set the cup in the sink. "I told you. I have to go to the B&B."

Katie was growing impatient with her *schweschder's* secrets. "I thought today was your day off?"

"It is, but I promised Bess I'd go into town with her. She wants to pick up some new fabric to make new drapes for one of the guest rooms, and I told her I'd go with her."

Katie walked over to the sink and stood beside Rose. "You were complaining to me about how I've neglected you since you gotten here. And now I haven't seen you a full day since. You're always running off somewhere. Is there something going on with you that I need to know about? Are you up to something?"

Rose placed a hand on her *schweschder's* shoulder. "*Nee.* Everything is fine. I have things to do, and you should be happy since that will allow you to spend more time with Caleb. I'm happy with my job. Bess has been very kind to me."

Katie scrunched up her face. "You call her by her first name? She will be my *aenti* when I marry Caleb, and I don't even call her by her first name."

Rose smiled. "I suppose that's because we have become more like friends."

Katie nearly choked on her *kaffi*. "Friends? She's so much older than you are, Rose."

"The age a person is has no bearing on whether they will make a *gut* friend. Besides, she's only turning fifty this year. That isn't so old."

Katie felt a little jealousy rise up in her. "I suppose not. When you get home, will you have time to work on the wedding dresses? I'd like to finish them so that is out of the way."

Rose smiled. "Of course we can. But you know the wedding is still several months away. You don't have to have everything done now."

"Come harvest season, everyone will be too busy with canning bees and the like, so I want all the big details taken care of now."

Rose hugged her *schweschder,* and then walked out the door. She understood wanting to ready everything for the wedding, but Rose hoped that she would be planning for her own wedding soon as well.

ಬಂಛ

Rose wasn't keen on riding into town with Jessup driving, but Bess had trusted him with her mare. She didn't want to ride in the front of the buggy, but Bess had insisted she needed to sit in the back so she could stretch out to avoid getting queasy. Rose felt a little awkward around the *mann* with which her own *schweschder* used to be betrothed, but Bess trusted him, so she didn't argue. Even though she knew it was a sham and that her parents had forced Katie into the engagement, it still felt odd being around Jessup. She didn't dislike him the way Katie had at the time, but there was something odd about his visits to the B&B. This was his second trip in three weeks, and Bess had told her he was here on business. But now Rose learned he would return at the end of the week with his *kinner*. If Rose didn't know any better, she'd think Jessup King was looking to move to the community.

When they reached the outskirts of town, Rose admired many shops that were run by the Amish. Everything from a bakery to a quilt shop, and even a shop that sold antiques and wares homemade by the Amish in the community graced the main road. Rose was mesmerized every time she caught a glimpse of the town-folk, and often wondered what their lives were like.

Jessup parked the buggy in front of the bank, claiming he had some business to take care of. He'd suggested they meet at the diner around the corner as soon as they'd finished getting fabric.

"I won't be long," Jessup called over his shoulder. "I'll meet you in twenty minutes."

Rose wondered what sort of business he might have at the bank, but it only furthered her assumption that he was planning to move to the community. Why would he want to live in the same community as Katie? Unless he had plans to try to win her back. Would he stoop so low as to try to break up Katie and Caleb after all this time had passed? He'd have to be a fool to try.

Chapter 24

Caleb pulled his buggy across Main Street and parked in front of the hardware store. He'd recognized his *aenti* Bess's buggy parked at the bank across the street and thought it odd. He walked across traffic and patted Buttercup on the head. She responded with a whinny and bobbed her head, nudging Caleb affectionately with her nose.

Caleb gave her nose another pat, and then walked around the corner to get an ice cream cone from the diner. The only time he indulged in the sweet treat was during his summertime trips to town, and it was warm enough today to make him crave the frozen treat. As he rounded the corner, he glanced inside and noticed Rose sitting at one of the tables. She was with a *mann,* and giggled like someone who was on a date and flirting. When the waitress walked by the table, the *mann* turned to get her attention. She tore a sheet off the pad of paper in her hand and handed it to *Jessup King!*

Even though the *mann* Caleb now stared at was beardless, it was indeed Jessup King. Was he courting Rose? Was that the reason for shaving his beard? Katie had complained to him that Rose had been running off lately and spending a lot of time at the B&B—even on her days off. Why would his *aenti* allow the two of them to take her buggy into town for a date? He would get to the bottom of this, but Caleb would not engage in a public confrontation. He would wait and go over to the B&B to talk with his *aenti* later. Right now, he'd suddenly lost his appetite for that ice cream cone.

ৰ০৫৪

Noah waved to his cousin who had just crossed the street and walked toward the hardware store. Standing in front of the diner, he wondered what had caused Caleb to stare through the window so intently. As he peered inside, his heart skipped a beat at the realization of what had caught Caleb's attention. Rose sat in the middle of the diner at a small table with an older *mann*—an un-bearded *mann*. If the *mann* wore no beard, he was unmarried. Who was he? Did his cousin know? Noah watched the two of them converse happily—almost as though they were on a date.

When he'd approached the diner from the feed store, Caleb's back had been to him and he'd been staring through the window of the diner. He hadn't gone in. He'd simply stood outside the window before jogging across the street to the hardware store. Caleb had seemed as unnerved as Noah was now, but he couldn't ask his cousin about it, or he would discover his feelings for Rose. His feelings that had obviously gone unrequited.

Noah walked away from the diner before Rose caught him staring through the window. He'd embarrassed himself enough by throwing himself on her twice, and now it seemed she was dating someone else. He wondered how long they'd been together, and why she hadn't mentioned it to him before they kissed? Was she unhappy with the *mann?* Judging from her laughter, he'd have to say she was not unhappy with him. He didn't think Rose was the type of girl to date more than one *mann* at a time, but it was possible he was wrong about that assumption.

৪৩৵

Bess returned from the bathroom and sat down at the table between Rose and Jessup.

"Jessup was just telling me the funniest story, Bess. You have to get him to tell you while I use the ladies' room. I'll be right back."

Jessup began to recount his story while Rose got up and went toward the back of the diner to reach the ladies' room. She wasn't real keen on using public restrooms, but she'd had too many refills of her soda-pop.

When she finished, she stood at the sink to wash her hands and examined herself in the large mirror as she did. She'd gotten a lot of sun lately while taking care of the celery patch for Katie, and she thought she was beginning to resemble the *Englisch* girls who wore a lot of makeup. She'd always tanned easily, and she thought she looked better with a little color on her face. It seemed to override the dullness that normally paled her.

ဆာ

By the time they arrived back at the B&B, Rose felt like she'd put in a full day already. She wanted to stop by and visit with Noah, but she'd promised Katie she would work on sewing the wedding dresses when she returned. She'd had fun, which surprised her. She'd never thought she could actually have fun talking to Jessup, but he'd had some funny stories about the constant antics of his *kinner,* and it was quite entertaining listening to him. She could see that he genuinely loved his *kinner,* and Rose thought that was a *gut* quality—one she'd missed when he was engaged to Katie.

ဆာ

"We need to talk about something serious, Rose, and this can't wait."

"At least let me get my sewing. We can talk then."

Katie didn't wait for her to return with her sewing. She followed closely on Rose's heals as she clomped up the stairs, exhaustion apparent in each step. She turned around midway, frowning at her *schweschder.*

"Katie, why are you following me? I'll be right down."

Katie continued to follow, causing Rose a great deal of irritation. "What is so important that you had to follow me up the stairs?"

"I know why you've been disappearing all the time. Why didn't you tell me you were seeing *someone?*"

Rose's heart fluttered with dread. She didn't want to say anything about her relationship with Noah until she was certain where it stood.

Katie scowled at Rose. "Your silence tells me it's true! Well, I forbid you to date Jessup King!"

Chapter 25

"You forbid me?"

Rose decided to play along. She had no idea what had made Katie think she was seeing Jessup, but it was the perfect cover-up until she could figure things out with Noah without her *schweschder* getting into her affairs like she was now.

"Yes, I forbid you. I decided to follow you to the B&B to see what was *really* causing you to run off all the time, and that's when I saw you getting into the buggy with Jessup. I know he's changed, but he made me miserable when I was forcibly engaged to him. Besides, I find it a little creepy that you would decide to date him. You aren't serious are you?"

Rose pressed her lips into a grim line. "And if I am? What then? Would you forbid me to marry him if I chose to do so? Honestly, I find it *creepy* that my own *schweschder* thinks she has to spy on me!"

Katie fumed. "It's obvious *someone* needs to keep tabs on you. Why would you even think to marry Jessup? Has he proposed to you?"

Rose remembered the heated proposal she'd received from Noah. Her cheeks warmed at the thought of it.

"I've been proposed to."

It wasn't a complete lie. She'd been proposed to—just not from Jessup.

Katie's eyes bulged and her mouth gaped.

"He proposed to you? Please tell me you told him no!"

Rose was almost enjoying this. It angered her that her *schweschder* would accuse of her of such a thing in the first place. But to believe it to be true was another thing altogether. She wasn't sure how long she could keep this up, but certainly long enough to teach Katie a lesson to stay out of her business. Katie had always tried to boss her. She never understood why, but she assumed it had everything to do with the fact that their parents controlled her so closely. It still surprised her that her parents had allowed Katie to remain in this community, but she suspected *Aenti* Nettie had had a lot to do with winning that argument.

"I didn't give my answer."

It was still the truth…

Katie breathed a sigh of relief. The thought of Rose marrying Jessup was too much for Katie to accept. She *had* to stop it from happening—for Rose's sake—and for her own. It would be awkward, to say the least, to see her *schweschder* marry him.

"Then you still have time to break it off."

Rose bristled. "What if I don't want to break it off with him? What if I love him?"

"Do you love him?"

Rose thought about Noah. There was no denying her love for him.

"I do love him. Very much."

Katie drew in a quick breath. "Does he feel the same about you?"

With the way Rose had responded to Noah's proposal, she wasn't sure if he would still have her. It broke her heart to even think about it, but she had to face the fact that even though she loved him deeply, his proposal may not have been sincere. He'd practically taken it back afterward. She wished she could be sure of his feelings for her, but the truth was, she couldn't.

"I hope he does," Rose whispered.

Katie furrowed her brow. "What do you mean, you *hope* he does? You seem so sure of your own feelings. Why aren't you so sure of his?"

Rose was confused over Katie's sudden change of attitude toward her *relationship* with Jessup. It almost seemed she was being supportive of it.

"I really don't feel like discussing this anymore. Can we work on sewing the dresses for your wedding, and just forget about this other stuff?"

"No, Rose. It's obvious you're upset. I only want to help you."

Rose grabbed the wedding attendant dress from the peg in the corner of the room and headed back downstairs.

"Rose please let me help you," Katie said as she followed her *schweschder* down the steps.

Rose turned on her heels so quickly that Katie ran into her. "If you really want to help me, you'll drop it and forget I ever said anything."

Their conversation had gotten so out of control that Rose, herself, was becoming confused by it all. She no longer thought it amusing that Katie had mistaken her love for Noah and transferred it to her suspicion over Jessup. Truth be told, she was heartbroken at the moment, and she didn't know how to make it right. Only seeing Noah and being in his arms would make things right, and she didn't see that happening.

"How am I supposed to forget that my *schweschder* is in *lieb* with Jessup King?"

Rose fought tears, and turned her back to Katie so she could get control of her emotions. She busied herself at the sink making a fresh pot of *kaffi* even though it was much too warm to drink it. She needed something to keep her hands busy and her mind off of Noah long enough to figure a way out this new mess she'd brought on herself.

Rose suddenly turned toward Katie, who'd sat at the kitchen table and had begun to pin the hem of her blue wedding dress.

"It no longer matters because I don't think he returns my feelings."

"Why would he propose if he didn't love you?"

Rose bit her lower lip. "He proposed to you when he didn't love you."

Katie stood up and walked over to the sink and placed her arm around Rose. "That was different because I didn't love him either."

Rose couldn't hold in her emotions any longer. With her *schweschder's* arms wrapped tightly around her, she began to weep softly. "Why do *menner* think it's alright to ask a woman to marry them when they don't really mean it? After he proposed, he practically took it back. He said he didn't mean for it to come out. That he had only said it because he was so caught up in our kiss that he hadn't thought it out."

Katie pushed Rose from her arms so she could look her in the eye. "He kissed you on the mouth?"

Rose remembered her kisses with Noah with a far-off look in her eyes. "*Jah.* And it was *wunderbaar.*"

Katie shook. Not once during her engagement to Jessup had he kissed her on the mouth.

Chapter 26

"I have something I have to tell you!" Katie was nearly out of breath when she ran out to meet Caleb after he pulled his buggy into the yard.

"I have something I have to tell you too, and it can't wait."

Katie climbed into the buggy and settled in next to Caleb. "My news first, please. I don't think I can wait another second to tell you."

"Jessup is back in town and I saw him at the diner with Rose," Caleb blurted out.

Katie's eyes grew wide. "Then it's true!"

Caleb dropped the reins. "What is true?"

Katie held back the tears that threatened to spill from her eyes. "He proposed marriage to her."

"Jessup King proposed marriage to your *schweschder*, Rose?"

Katie let loose the tears. "*Jah*, and he broke her heart. As soon as he proposed, he took it back. She really loves him."

"What do you mean he took back his proposal?"

"That's what she told me. She said that he proposed to her right after kissing her full on the mouth. He never once kissed me on the mouth. This is serious."

Caleb raised an eyebrow. "He never kissed you on the mouth? Really?"

Katie scowled. "Why do you say that like you're surprised?"

"I'm not as surprised as I am happy about it. It means I was your first real kiss, *jah?*"

"*Jah,* you were."

"*Das gut.*"

Katie wiped her tears and smiled at her betrothed. "Let's put our concentration back on my dear *schweschder.* What are we going to do about this?"

Caleb thought about it for a minute. "I think I need to have a talk with the Bishop again, but I'd like to give Jessup a chance to explain his side of the story."

"He has nothing to explain. He has gone and done what he threatened to do. I can't believe we thought he'd changed. He hasn't changed. He was biding his time until he could lure my *schweschder* into his plan of revenge. He gave us his word he would not pursue her, and he broke that promise. And now he's broken Rose's heart along with that promise. He's a horrible *mann,* and you need to tell the Bishop of his actions right away."

Caleb put his arm around Katie to calm her.

"Is it possible that Rose misunderstood him?"

"You didn't see how upset she was. Rose has always been very level-headed. We've seen first-hand what Jessup King is capable of."

Caleb rubbed his hand across his smooth chin. "It doesn't make any sense to me. When I saw them at the diner earlier, they looked happy. Rose was laughing; Jessup was laughing. They were having a *gut* time. I don't understand what could have happened in the last hour to make him change his mind about her."

Katie sniffled. "He didn't change his mind about her. He never cared about her in the first place, just like with me. The only difference between the two is that I didn't fall in lieb with him, but Rose did. And he took advantage of her vulnerability. He should never have kissed her on the mouth. That sort of kiss should be saved for the *mann* you are to be married to. He has taken that special first-kiss from her and she can never get that back. He should suffer excommunication for his behavior."

Caleb was trying to see this from Katie's point of view, but there was still something that was nagging him about this. "That seems a little harsh, don't you think? Perhaps we should hear him out first. We talked to him last time, and his remorse seemed genuine."

Katie leered at Caleb. "An evil *mann* will let honey drip from his tongue."

"I don't think we should assume he's become evil until I have a talk with him first so we can get to the bottom of this. There *has* to be a logical explanation, and we owe it to Rose *and* to Jessup to find out what that is before we jump to conclusions."

Katie wiped her face on her apron. "What are you waiting for? Let's go find out why he did this to Rose."

Caleb pulled Katie's hands into his own and looked her in the eye. "I think you should stay here with Rose. She needs you. I'm going to go over and get Noah to help me. I don't want to approach Jessup alone, and I think Noah would be a *gut* person to take with me. He's always been very level-headed. I think it's best if I have another *mann* with me when I defend your *schweschder's* honor."

Katie sighed. "But Noah doesn't even know Rose *or* Jessup. How can he help if he doesn't know who he's up against?"

Caleb kissed Katie's hands. "I think it is better that Noah doesn't know either Rose or Jessup. That way he can be neutral in case I get a little too heated."

Katie cuddled him. "I think that's wise."

Caleb kissed Katie on the forehead, and then hugged her. "It's getting dark. I'm going to stop by Noah's place on the way home and fill him in on what's going on. We will probably go over to the B&B first thing in the morning and talk to Jessup. I'll come over after and let you know how it went. In the meantime, go spend some time with Rose."

"*Danki*. I don't know how I would have managed this without your help. I know I only met Noah briefly at the meal after church before he disappeared, but thank him for me. I appreciate whatever the two of you can do to fix this."

Katie waved to Caleb as he pulled the buggy out of the yard, and then she went in the *haus* to comfort Rose. She called out to her, searching the upstairs, the yard and even the barn, but Rose was gone.

Chapter 27

Rose stood in the grass at the end of the dock and watched mindlessly as fireflies swarmed around her. The night air was humid and warm, only a slight breeze bringing relief as the draft floated up her dress. Every minute that ticked by was another minute that Noah was not with her. She didn't hold out much hope that he would show up, but it remained in the back of her mind, tucked away where she refused to acknowledge it.

Not feeling up to catching fireflies, Rose walked to the end of the dock and lowered herself into the spot in which Noah usually waited for her while she took a boat ride. She hadn't been out on the boat in nearly a week, and she found that she lacked the desire to do so even now. Sadly, it only held amusement as long as she knew Noah was sitting in this very spot waiting for her. Without him, everything paled in comparison.

Rose kicked at the water, sending ripples across the pond. It reminded her of how much Noah liked to skip stones across it. Would everything she did remind her of Noah, or would she eventually forget him just as he seemed to have forgotten her?

Perhaps it's time to go back home to Nappanee.

♏⁓♑

Noah was just getting ready to head out to the dock at the B&B when his cousin, Caleb, drove his buggy up the drive to his *haus*. He'd planned to clear the air with Rose and tell her he loved her enough to marry her. Unsure of what he'd seen earlier in the diner, he decided to give her a chance to explain why she was with the older *mann*. Perhaps there was a logical explanation, and he was a relative. Either way, he loved her, and he was ready to commit if she would have him. Now he would have to postpone that meeting, depending on how long his cousin planned to stay.

Caleb jumped down from the buggy and held a hand out to his cousin. "*Wie gehts,* Noah."

Noah took his hand. "What brings you out here this time of night? Shouldn't you be taking a buggy ride with your betrothed?"

Caleb chuckled. "I wish I was. Even going home and cleaning the horse-stalls would be more fun than what I have on my plate right now."

Noah gave his cousin a concerned pat on the back. "What could be troubling you so much? You are engaged; you should be happy all the time."

"I'm very happy with Katie. It's her *schweschder*, Rose, that is causing concern."

At the mention of Rose, Noah's heart fluttered.

"What did she do that has you so concerned?"

Caleb leaned up against the porch railing. "It's not so much what she did as what Jessup King did to upset her."

The thought of someone hurting Rose sent anger through Noah. He was almost afraid to ask the question he knew he needed to. "What did he do to her?"

Caleb shot a look of concern to his cousin. He'd never known him to talk through gritted teeth before. It was almost as though Noah had a vested interest in Rose's well-being, but that would be impossible since he didn't even know her.

"It seems he asked her to marry him and then took it back."

Noah collapsed against the porch-rail, and caught himself so he wouldn't fall back. "He asked her to marry him? When?"

Caleb looked at his cousin with concern. "Are you able to handle news of the community, Noah? Maybe I shouldn't have relied on you so soon."

Noah shook his head. "I lost my footing is all. Is this Jessup an older fellow?"

"*Jah.* How did you know?"

Noah clenched his jaw. "I saw them in the diner today. They looked happy to me."

Caleb did a double-take toward Noah. "How do you know what Rose looks like?"

Clearing his throat, Noah chose his words carefully. "I spoke to her after church on Sunday."

It wasn't a lie. But it wasn't the entire truth either.

Caleb ran his hand through his hair and replaced his hat. "I'm not sure when everything happened, but I saw them in the diner this afternoon too. They did look like they were having a pleasant conversation. So I suppose it happened between then and an hour ago. Either way, he took back his proposal, and it seems he broke her heart."

That statement hit Noah too close to home. *He'd* been the one to propose and retrieve it. Had *he* broken Rose's heart? Or had she been counting on the proposal from Jessup too? Did he even propose? Noah certainly was eager to find out.

"I came over here to see if you would go with me to talk with Jessup tomorrow so we could get some answers. I want to know what he's up to with Rose. He'd warned Katie and me a while back that he intended on pursuing Rose out of spite, and I want to know if that's what he's up to."

Noah wanted answers more than Caleb could possibly understand. He loved Rose, and he thought she loved him too. But after seeing her in the diner with Jessup, and now hearing he may have proposed to her, Noah was worried he may have misjudged her character. Was it possible that Caleb's visit tonight had spared him from going to Rose at the pond and making a fool of himself?

"*Jah,* I will go with you. Do you think there's much truth to this proposal from Jessup?"

Caleb shrugged. "I have no idea. But I hope not for her sake. What baffles me the most is why Rose would allow herself to get involved with him to the point he could break her heart. I don't understand how or when she could have fallen in love with the *mann.*"

"She said she was in love with him?"

Caleb nodded.

Noah shuddered. If Rose was in love with Jessup, then why had she kissed *him* the way she had when they were together?

Chapter 28

Noah shuffled to the kitchen for some *kaffi.* After such a restless night, he needed something to perk him up. Because nothing could make him forget that the woman he loved had been proposed to by another *mann,* he wished Caleb had never told him.

After several hours of tossing about trying to sleep, Noah had all but convinced himself it had been a mistake to re-enter the community. He felt he'd been better off staying hidden in the shadows of the community where nothing could hurt him. But he couldn't regret meeting Rose, or she might be dead and gone, consumed by Goose Pond just as Emma had been.

Striking a match, Noah lit the pilot light of the gas stove, turned on the burner and set the percolator over the flame. He leaned against the sink wondering how things had gotten so out of control in his life. Life was supposed to be simple for Amish, wasn't it? How then, was his life beginning to feel so tangled and complicated? At the end of the week, his *daed* was expecting him for dinner. Was he even ready for that? He'd realized he may not have been ready to fall in love with Rose either. Everything was happening so fast all of a sudden that his mind had not had the proper amount of time to process it all.

The clip-clop of a horse and the sound of turning buggy wheels brought Noah's gaze toward the small window above the sink. Caleb had arrived early. He could only assume he was eager to get some answers, but Noah was no longer certain he wanted to know.

Sometimes what you don't know can't hurt you.

Caleb gave a quick warning knock at the back door, and then entered. "I know it's early, but I wanted to get this over with. If I know Jessup King, he'll slip out of town and we will miss the chance to confront him about Rose."

The mere mention of her name sent prickles of agony coursing down his spine. Bubbles of dark *kaffi* pushed up into the clear, glass percolator at the top of the tall pot on the stove. Noah turned off the burner, not caring that he'd be drinking weak brew. He was too tired to worry about steeping his morning beverage to perfection. He wanted to get this over with more than his cousin could ever know. His stomach roiled as he took his first sip. Would he be able to face Jessup without a physical confrontation? Right now he wasn't so sure about it.

Noah gulped the last of the still-hot *kaffi,* not caring that it burned his tongue. "Let's go," he growled.

Caleb held the door for his cousin. "Why are you in such a bad mood this morning?"

Noah waved him off. "Nothing. Just didn't get much sleep last night. I have a lot on my mind."

Caleb turned before climbing into the buggy.

"I'm sorry. If you're not up to this, I can go alone."

Noah looked at him sternly. *"Nee.* I want to go. Why don't we walk over? We can go through the back, around the pond."

Caleb agreed it would be quicker to avoid the traffic on the main road just to get to what seemed like was just around the curve from Noah's place.

They walked in silence the short distance to the back of the B&B. Noah eyed the dock as they approached. His heart sank at the thought of the kisses he'd shared with Rose, the kisses that had meant everything to him.

As they neared the back door, Caleb spotted a taxi-cab coming up the side road toward the B&B.

Caleb sped up his walk. "Jessup must be leaving. We need to hurry and catch him."

They entered through the back door and made their way to the parlor. Caleb stopped in his tracks when he saw that Jessup's arms were wrapped tightly around a woman who was clearly not Rose. He was passionately kissing her full on the mouth.

A strangled gasp escaped Caleb's lips.

Startled, the couple broke apart, the faces of each of them turning bright red. But more shocking than the kiss was the fact that the woman he'd been passionately kissing was *Aenti* Bess.

Noah reacted before Caleb could process what he'd seen. Noah charged toward Jessup, pushing him against the wall near the front door.

Caleb watched it all as though in slow motion. His brain told him he'd seen Jessup kissing *Aenti* Bess—on the mouth—passionately. Had he imagined it? Watching Noah confronting Jessup, and hearing his *aenti* rushing to the *mann's* defense told him he hadn't imagined it at all.

"How dare you take advantage of *mei aenti* after proposing to Rose! What kind of *mann* are you?"

Noah held Jessup against the wall with his forearm pressed against his chest. Bess tried to get between them. "Let him go, Noah."

Jessup fought to catch his breath. "I didn't ask Rose to marry me. I asked Bess to marry me."

Noah released him. His heart was beating so fast, he had to take a deep breath to calm himself.

Caleb stepped forward. "What are you talking about? We saw you yesterday at the diner in town with Rose. The two of you seemed pretty cozy. She told Katie you proposed to her and then took it back."

Bess cupped her arm in Jessup's and held a warning hand out to her nephews, letting them know to back off. "I was with them at the diner yesterday. I must have been in the bathroom when you walked by.

I'm not sure why Rose would say that Jessup proposed to her, because he proposed to *me*."

Caleb reached out a hand to Jessup. "I guess congratulations would be in order here. Sorry for the misunderstanding, but what about..." he lowered his voice to a whisper. "The *age* difference between the two of you."

Bess pursed her lips, and eyed Noah who'd stood by without uttering a word.

Jessup cleared his throat. "I know that Katie thought I was in my mid-thirties, but I'm really in my mid-forties. I led her to believe I was younger than I am because I was embarrassed about the age difference between the two of us. But now I don't have to hide my age anymore. Bess is only a few years older than I am, but I find that comforting. We are happy, and I hope in time you will be able to accept our union. We are to be married at the end of the week when I return with my *kinner*. We will be living at the B&B."

Caleb's heart softened at the look of love in his *aenti's* eyes. It was obvious she was happy, and he had no right to judge her for wanting what everyone wanted. It was her choice and he would respect it. "I hope you will extend us an invitation to the wedding."

"I was going to tell everyone at dinner on Friday at your *daed's haus.*" She aimed her statement at Noah.

Noah relaxed at the thought of his *daed* inviting him to a *familye* dinner. That meant he was finally ready to mend the rift between them.

Caleb pulled off his hat and scratched his head as though deep in thought. "There's one thing I don't understand. If Jessup didn't propose to Rose, who did?"

Noah swallowed the lump of nerves constricting his throat and looked into his cousin's waiting eyes. "I did."

Chapter 29

"What?" everyone, including Jessup, asked in unison.

Caleb raised an eyebrow. "What do you mean? *You did*? You're the one that proposed to Rose and broke her heart? Why would you do such a thing? You don't even know her."

A honk sounded from outside. Jessup picked up his suitcase. "As much as I'd like to stay and hear all about this, I must go. I've got a lot of packing to do in the next two days before I return. *Gut daag,* I'll see the two of you later."

Caleb and Noah ignored Jessup as Bess walked him out to the waiting taxi-cab.

The two of them sat down on the landing of the wide stairwell, Noah on the upper riser.

"I do know Rose, and I love her. I don't know why she would think I took back my proposal. She's the one that walked away from me without giving me an answer. For the past two days I thought she didn't want anything to do with me. And after the fun we've had in each other's company, I've felt awful about not seeing her. Then when I saw her with Jessup yesterday at the diner, I thought it was over between us for certain."

Caleb shook his head, still trying to process this new turn of events. "How did the two of you meet? Have you been seeing her all summer?"

"We met at the pond one night. She fell in and I pulled her out of the water. She thinks I saved her life, but it was *my* life that was saved that night. If not for her, I'd still be wallowing in the self-destructive pity that took me from the community. I owe her my life."

"So you asked her to marry you?"

"I asked her to marry me because I fell in love with her. We have fun together, and we can talk about anything. She understands me and accepts me with unconditional love."

"Noah, she thinks you took back your proposal."

Noah sighed. "I apologized for blurting it out. I think I told her I proposed to her because I was caught up in the moment of our kiss—that it spurred the proposal. She must think I didn't really mean it. I have to talk to her and get her to understand that I didn't take it back."

Noah jumped up and walked over to the check-in desk in the front parlor of the B&B and grabbed a notepad. He scribbled a quick note on the page, folded it and handed it to Caleb. "Will you make sure Rose gets this? I'm going to stay here and wait for *Aenti*

Bess to come back in and talk to her. I think I have a way to make things right with Rose."

Caleb slapped his cousin on the back. "I'll do whatever I can to help. I will be praying for you. Don't mess it up this time. Rose is a *gut* match for you."

"*Danki.* That means a lot that you support me on this."

Caleb and Noah walked back to the kitchen. Caleb left, and Noah poured himself a fresh cup of *kaffi.* It was going to be a long day.

ഇരു

Caleb knocked on the back door and waited for Katie to answer. Instead, she hollered that it was open. As he entered the kitchen, Rose and Katie sat at the table eating breakfast.

"Won't you join us?" Katie asked him.

"*Nee.* Noah asked me to give this to you."

He handed the note to Rose. She opened it and read the contents, a smile forming on her lips.

Katie looked between Rose and Caleb. "Why is Noah sending notes to my *schweschder?*"

Rose jumped up from the table happily and bolted from the room. Katie cringed at the stomping she'd made as she ran up the stairs.

Katie turned to Caleb. "Are you going to tell me what is going on? What happened with Bess? And why is your cousin, Noah, sending notes to Rose? He doesn't even know her."

Caleb found it difficult to hide his smile. "Jessup didn't propose to Rose. Noah did."

Chapter 30

Katie spit her *kaffi* across the table. Choking and coughing, she tried to speak.

Caleb patted her on the back. "Are you alright?"

Katie nodded her head. "Why did Noah propose to her? What about Jessup? Why didn't she deny it when I asked her about Jessup?"

Caleb took the cup from Katie's hand and set it aside. "There's more. Are you ready for it?"

Katie nodded. How much more news could there be?

"Jessup asked *Aenti* Bess to marry him."

Katie pushed back her chair, scraping it against the wood floor. "We have to go to the Bishop. We can't let him take advantage of that poor woman. Doesn't Jessup King know how to prey on anyone his own age?"

Caleb suppressed a smile. "Turns out, he's only three years younger than my *aenti*. He led you to believe he was in his mid-thirties, but he's about eleven years older than he told you he was."

Katie couldn't breathe. If what Caleb said was true, she'd nearly been tricked into marrying a *mann* twenty-one years her senior. Leaning over the sink, she turned on the faucet and splashed cold water over her face several times. Was it possible to wash off disgust?

She looked back at Caleb, her face dripping.

"Do you have anything else to tell me as long as I'm hanging my head over the sink? I think I'll stay here just in case I lose my breakfast."

Caleb stepped up to the sink and placed a comforting arm around his betrothed. He understood how she was feeling. He remembered how sick he felt when he found out she was promised to Jessup. But that seemed like a million years ago now. "I have no more shocking news to tell you. That was it."

Relieved, Katie wiped her face on the linen tea-towel hanging from the handle on the stove.

"Tell me about Rose and Noah."

Caleb pulled Katie into his arms and kissed her lightly on top of her head. "I will later. Right now, I just want to hold you."

Chapter 31

Rose lay across her bed staring at the words on the note from Noah. He'd requested a meeting with her on the dock at the B&B at nine o'clock. Several thoughts ran through her head; everything from Noah declaring his love for her all over again and asking her to marry him, to the possibility that he wanted to see her so he could break things off with her. At first, she'd thought the letter to be a positive one, but now she couldn't be sure. The only hint she had was his signature: *Love, Noah.*

Had it meant that he loved her, or was it simply a polite salutation? Either way, she would find out at the end of the day. Since today was her day off at the B&B, Rose decided to spend the time finishing her dress for Katie's wedding. She'd promised her *schweschder* she would have it done by the end of the week, and there would not be another day when she would have the entire day to fill. If she didn't keep herself busy today, it would drive her mad thinking about her meeting later with Noah. Whatever his intentions were, she would not let him go without telling him how much she loved him. She would risk everything on the chance that he truly loved her in return.

ꙮꙮ

Noah lit the candles in the Mason jars he'd used to line the dock at the B&B. Bess had loaned them to him, stating it would create a romantic walkway for Rose to meet him at the end of the dock. Stars twinkled in the black, cloudless sky, and the thumbnail moon angled itself amidst of the canopy of stars. Noah couldn't have asked *Gott* to provide a more perfect setting for this special night with Rose.

ꙮꙮ

Rose pulled her neatly-pressed, pink dress over her head. It was the prettiest color she owned. She didn't twist her hair up in the back, and she left her *kapp* on its hook. She looked into the oval mirror that hung from the back of her bureau admiring her long hair. She hoped Noah would approve of such boldness since he didn't seem to mind the previous times they'd spent together. For her, it was a way to relay the message that she was giving herself to him.

After learning of Jessup's proposal of marriage to Bess, Rose felt more confident than ever that love was in her own future as well. She was happy for her friend, and knowing that if even Bess could find love at such a late stage in life, surely Rose had an even better chance for the same in her own young life.

Rose tip-toed down the stairs in her bare feet. She didn't want Katie to stop her and reprimand her for not wearing her *kapp*. She knew her *schweschder* was getting ready to take a buggy ride with Caleb, but she couldn't wait for them to leave or she would be late for her special meeting with the *mann* she loved.

Breathing a sigh of relief at having made it out of the *haus* without being seen by Katie, Rose walked swiftly through the cool grass toward the B&B. The closer she came to the dock, she noticed the lighted jars along the edge of the dock. Her heart leapt with joy, for she knew that he loved her. He wouldn't have gone to the trouble to create something so romantic if he didn't want the night to be more special than the previous nights they'd spent at the dock.

Then she saw him standing at the end of the dock. His smile told her he'd been waiting for her. She walked between the candles that flickered in the Mason jars, keeping her focus on Noah, who stood patiently waiting for her. Neither of them spoke for fear of breaking the romantic spell between them.

Rose stood before him suddenly feeling shy and unsure of herself. Was she really bold enough to get what she wanted? She *had* to be. Even though she was scared of rejection, she couldn't let anything stand between them any longer or it would destroy her.

Closing the space between them, Rose coiled her fingers in his royal blue shirt and used it pull him low enough until his lips met hers. She deepened the kiss when she wrapped her arms around his neck. Noah held her close, lifting her slightly until she stood on her tip-toes.

"I love you, Rose," Noah said between kisses. "I want to marry you."

Happy tears formed in Rose's eyes. "I want to be your *fraa.*"

Noah let out a heavy sigh of relief. "I'm so glad. I've been here for more than an hour going over what I would say to convince you in case you said no."

"How could I say no to you? I love you."

Rose looked down at their feet where a jar of fireflies was glowing brightly. She reached down to pick it up and examine the contents.

"How did you manage to get so many?"

Noah chuckled. "Like I said, I've been here for over an hour."

"One is trying to escape. It looks like you twisted the lid on crooked. The cheesecloth is loose at the top."

Rose strained to untwist the lid, which seemed to be stuck, when her elbow knocked into Noah's chest with enough force to make him lose his balance. He teetered backward and then fell into the pond with a big splash.

Rose held her breath until he surfaced.

She reached a hand out to him, but he boosted himself up from the end of the dock.

"I'm so sorry. I didn't mean to push you in."

Noah laughed heartily. "Maybe I should throw you in and then we'd be even."

Rose squealed.

"You're lucky I'm a gentleman, or I would."

Not caring that he was dripping wet with pond water, Rose pulled Noah into another deep kiss, and his response to her was just what she'd hoped for. Magically, fireflies swarmed around them, but Rose noticed they'd come out from the jar she still held in her hand.

"Oh no. They got away. I didn't mean to let them go. You worked so hard to catch them."

Noah leaned in and kissed her ear and whispered to her. "It's alright, we can catch more. Don't you know, Rose, there is no place I'd rather be than here with you, chasing fireflies."

The End

Don't miss the sneak peek chapters of
A Sheriff's Legacy: Book One
(Christian, Historical Romance)
Please turn the page to read the two sample chapters.

A Sheriff's Legacy: Book One

WRITTEN BY
SAMANTHA JILLIAN BAYARR

CHAPTER ONE

May, 1885
Tombstone, Arizona

Wells Fargo stage robbed. Stop. Outlaws unaccounted for. Stop. Clayton Fisher gunned down. Stop. Critical condition. Stop.
Marshall Tucker.

Logan Fisher held the telegraph in his trembling fist as he exited the train onto the platform near Tombstone, Arizona. Although he'd said a quick prayer for his estranged father's recovery, he was still reluctant to go to the dying man's bedside. To be honest, he couldn't even be certain which side of the law his Pa had fallen on, and he was more interested in hunting down the outlaws than seeing his Pa again.

He hadn't seen the man for over fifteen years after he'd been dropped at the doorstep of his Aunt Mirabelle and Uncle William just after his Ma had died from a rattlesnake bite.

Pa had blamed him.

He'd even blamed himself.

The only one that hadn't blamed him was Ma.

She'd been bitten out on the prairie where she went searching for him that stormy afternoon in June. Pa had warned him time and again to stay away from the small cave etched into the rocky cliffs that bordered their spread of land, but he'd only ducked inside when the storm began to stir up into a thick veil of dust that shielded the distance between him and the ranch.

When he heard Ma's cry straining against the dust storm, his emotions flared. He was twelve years old, and didn't want to be followed like a small child. But Ma knew him too well. She knew exactly where to find him, and now she was in distress from the storm. When he reached the mouth of the cave, he spotted her petite frame lying on the ground some distance from him.

Pulling up his kerchief from around his neck to cover his mouth and nose, he stretched his spindly legs toward her. As he came upon her, that's when he saw the snake. It reared its head only for a moment before slithering away.

Logan knelt at his Ma's side looking for the bite. Blood stained the dust-covered bloomers that modestly disguised her calves.

Then he saw the bite marks.

Both of them.

Logan reached for the pocket knife that Pa had given him for his twelfth birthday and scored both bites. After sucking the venom from the wounds and spitting it on the ground, he lifted his canteen to his mouth to rinse the venom from his lips, and then offered a drink to his weak mother.

She looked up at him; her hazel eyes had gone dark.

"I love you, son."

He grabbed her limp hand in his. "I'm so sorry Ma. I'll never disobey you again. I promise. Please don't die!"

Her eyes fluttered. "It's not your fault, Logan. You're a good boy. Just promise me you'll take care of your Pa."

"I will, Ma. But you promise me you won't die."

"I promise."

Her eyes closed and her breathing was shallow. She didn't even cough against the dust swirling around her cheeks. Logan pulled his kerchief from around his neck and covered his Ma's face against the dust whirling around.

Knowing the doc's cabin was on the other side of the rocky ridge; he judged the distance to be shorter than that of his own cabin. He hoisted his Ma's thin frame into a sitting position and cupped his arms under her armpits and began to drag her backward in the loose clay toward the doc's cabin. Each laboring step filled his lungs with more dust, but he didn't stop to cough; he knew his Ma was failing fast.

When the cabin came into view, he began hollering for the doc, his mouth filling with dust. His eyes were dry and his lashes were coated with the same clay dust that nearly covered his Ma's body. Just when he thought he couldn't pull her another foot, the doc was at his side. The older man flung his Ma over his shoulder like a sack of feed and took her into his cabin.

Logan ran to get his Pa, leaving his Ma with the doc. When he found his Pa in the barn, he told him the story in between coughs. He'd never forget the look in his Pa's eyes when he pulled the horse whip from the tack room and tanned his hide before riding off toward the doc's cabin. Logan ignored the pain of his backside as he flung himself bareback over one of the geldings and rode the reluctant horse through the calming storm. When he arrived at the doc's cabin, his Pa refused to let him see his Ma.

She died two hours later.

ⓈⓄⒸⓇ

Clayton Fisher hadn't spoken one word to his son since his wife's death. After her burial, Clayton took his son and all of his belongings to the train station and boarded him for Texas. He'd wired ahead to his sister Mirabelle and her husband, William, who would be waiting at the other side for Logan. Over the years, his Pa sent word of his whereabouts and always included several paper notes to cover the cost of his room and board. But there was never a personal word from father to son. Logan became bitter until his aunt and uncle slowly broke through the rigid barrier with scripture and regular church-going.

His aunt and uncle had become like parents to him. Logan had tried to help his uncle keep their small cattle ranch from falling on hard times, but it was a failing ranch when he'd arrived. Though they were unable to turn a profit after the first year he'd began boarding with them, they were able to keep food on the table with the few head of cattle they managed.

When Logan turned seventeen, the fever claimed his Aunt Belle and Uncle Will. After laying them to rest, he joined a band of cowboys who made their living as bounty hunters. He roamed the countryside with the posse tracking wanted men for a profit. He grew up on the open range, though he'd become a man at the age of twelve the day his Ma died.

CHAPTER TWO

After fetching his horse, Buckeye, from the ventilated stock cars at the rear of the train, Logan pointed the already tired horse toward Tombstone, and settled in for the long ride to the mining town where his Pa waited for him. First stop in town would be the livery to board his horse for at least a day, since the gelding would be tired from the long train ride and travel on foot to Tombstone.

The terrain was tough, with an abundance of deep ruts from wagon wheels jutting along the stretch of open land that isolated the mining town from the rest of civilization.

As the town came into view, Logan could see that it was bustling with activity. Even at a distance he could hear the noises of the busy town. He steered Buckeye down the main stretch of Allen Street, noting the shops and businesses, restaurants, and over-abundance of saloons. The boardwalk was filled with people of several races; miners, prospectors and wealthy town-folk mingled along the rowdy street going about their business as though they were in a hurry.

Logan hopped off of Buckeye in front of the OK Corral Feed & Livery Stable, and led the horse to a watering trough before entering the livery. The sign boasted ownership established by John Montgomery in 1881, and offered a number of services for horses and other livestock.

A tall, burly man greeted him with a handshake.

"What can I do for ya?"

"I could use a fresh horse, and board for mine for at least a day so he can rest from the long trip from Texas."

The livery owner accepted the silver pieces from Logan without question. But after signing his name in the ledger, the burly man gave him a once-over and tipped his hat respectfully.

"You here to see the Marshall?"

Logan nodded, hoping to avoid revealing his business to the stranger.

"You must be Clayton's boy. You look like him."

Assuming the man would not have addressed his Pa by his given name if he was an outlaw, he let his guard down a little. "Yes Sir, I am. Do you know where I can find him?"

The older man pointed to the opposite end of the boardwalk. "Doc's office is above the Crystal Palace at the corner of Fifth Street, on the second floor. But they're guarding Clay just outside of town past the fire house on Toughnut Street—near the mine. If you take Fifth Street south, it'll get you there."

Logan's heart skipped a beat. Maybe he was an outlaw after all. "Guarding him?"

"Of course, you'll have to stop by the Marshall's office first so Sheriff Daniels can escort you out there. You'll find the Marshall's office next to the doc."

Logan refrained from asking the man anymore questions, feeling unsure about what the answers might be. Instead, he took the man up on his offer of a fresh mount.

After tending to Buckeye, he saddled up and rode down to the Marshall's office to see about his Pa. He let the horse walk at a slow pace as he took in the many businesses along the way. The streets were bustling with noisy patrons and those conducting business along the busy stretch of the city.

Violet calico fluttering in the slight breeze caught the corner of Logan's eye. He tried to keep his focus on the task before him, but he couldn't help but feel drawn to the woman wearing it. Without even seeing her face, he sensed a familiarity that caused him to slow the horse to a near stand-still just long enough to bask in the unusual pull he felt coming from her. He kept his face forward as long as he could stand it, and then gazed upon her.

He tipped his hat to avoid her thinking he was gawking at her, but he couldn't help but stare. The breeze played with blond curls that framed her face, the rest of her hair lay at the base of her neck in a wind-blown chignon. As her lashes lifted in his direction, green eyes stared back at him, and her parasol didn't hide the glint of sunlight that sparkled in them. She smiled as he passed her, causing his heart to skip a beat. For a moment, he let his guard down long enough to feel. But as he looked down the road to his destination, his heart hardened again with dreaded anticipation of what he was about to encounter at the Marshall's office.

໐໐

Daisy Mae Pinkerton felt the hair on the back of her neck stand on end as she watched the handsome stranger ride through town. Though she was sure she had never seen him before, he boasted a familiarity that she just couldn't shake. Perched atop a large steed, he carried a rugged sort of brashness that gave him just enough edge to convince everyone but her.

As he approached, she averted her eyes until the last minute. When she set her gaze upon him, her heart fluttered in perfect rhythm with the folds of her dress that moved with the breeze. Her untamed hair danced along her face at just the right time to mask the color that had claimed her cheeks.

She saw vulnerability in his eyes, but his seat suggested otherwise. He rode with confidence, though his eyes revealed a hint of insecurity. His full lips parted for a moment from the clenched mien that preserved the scowl assailing his handsome face.

When he smiled back at her, the blue in his eyes softened.

Ducking into the mercantile, Daisy pulled a folded fan from the drawstring reticule that hung from her wrist so she could cool her heated cheeks. "It's warm out there today." She tried to disguise her embarrassment to Clarisse Prescott and her mother as they approached her.

"Good afternoon, Daisy," Mrs. Prescott said.

She nodded, hoping to avoid a lengthy conversation with the women that tended to gossip a bit too much.

Mrs. Prescott put a hand to Daisy's arm to halt her furious fanning. "Are you alright, dear?"

"I'm just a little warm from the walk over from the school house."

She couldn't tell the woman she was swooning over a rugged man that just rode down the street in front of her. She had learned a long time ago to keep a tight lid on anything of a private matter with Mrs. Prescott after she talked behind Maddie Hayes' back when her husband ran off and left her with two children. Instead of being the charitable woman she professed in church, she exploited her predicament.

Daisy, however, had been the one to lead the women's group in taking up a fund for the poor Mrs. Hayes to pay her passage back east to live with her parents. Daisy's Ma was no longer by her side, but her teachings remained etched in her brain like the Ten Commandments carved into the stone tablets. Her Ma had taught her to keep a tight rein on her mouth, and to keep people like Mrs. Prescott at an arm's length. She remained respectable toward the woman, but not overly friendly as to encourage gossip. As the school teacher, Daisy couldn't afford to soil her reputation by gossiping—or swooning over men—especially since her teaching contract didn't permit her to marry.

Clarisse was a different story altogether. She and Daisy had been friends since the day she and Pa rode into town when she accepted the two-year teaching contract and her Pa accepted his new flock at St. Paul's church.

Clarisse was nothing like her meddling mother who often embarrassed her. Whenever they conversed, they made certain that her mother was not within earshot of their conversation, lest she spread it around town. In Daisy's opinion, Mrs. Prescott was usually a harmless busy-body, but she just didn't seem to understand that sometimes her gossiping hurt others.

Daisy slighted her eyes and winked at Clarisse, letting her know she had a secret to tell her. The young woman drifted away from her mother's side long enough to whisper to her friend.

"If you're going to tell me about that beautiful man that just sauntered down the road, I already saw him through the window of the mercantile. I had to pretend I was looking at the bolts of fabric so Mama wouldn't catch me slighting my eyes toward the man."

Daisy raised her eyebrows at her friend's boldness.

Clarisse shrugged. "Just because I'm engaged to be married doesn't mean I've gone blind."

Suppressing a smile, Daisy huddled close to her friend. "He was beautiful, wasn't he? The man looked right into my very soul, Clarisse."

"No wonder you couldn't breathe when you walked in here."

Daisy took a deep breath. "The look in his blue eyes nearly took my breath away. I know it's not proper, but I have to go back outside to see where he goes. I *have* to know who he is."

Clarisse called to her mother across the room. "I'm going to take Daisy out to get some fresh air."

Her mother nodded and the two women stepped out onto the boardwalk. Across the street, they could see the man dismount his horse in front of the Crystal Palace. He walked up the stairway to the second floor, and removed his hat revealing thick, black hair just before entering the Marshall's office.

Daisy clutched Clarisse's arm. "Do you think he's here to join the posse that intends to put a stop to all the robberies? Surely he's not an outlaw, or he wouldn't have walked into the Marshall's office willingly."

Clarisse winked at her. "Why, Miss Daisy, are you gossiping?"

The two ladies giggled. "You sound exactly like your mother when you talk like that."

"It irritates me when she accuses others of doing the very thing at which she is so talented."